JOURNAL FOR THE STUDY OF THE OLD TESTAMENT
SUPPLEMENT SERIES
133

Editors
David J.A. Clines
Philip R. Davies

Editorial Board
Richard J. Coggins, Alan Cooper, Tamara C. Eskenazi,
J. Cheryl Exum, Robert P. Gordon, Norman K. Gottwald,
Andrew D.H. Mayes, Carol Meyers, Patrick D. Miller

JSOT Press
Sheffield

The Forsaken First-Born

A Study of a Recurrent Motif
in the Patriarchal Narratives

Roger Syrén

Journal for the Study of the Old Testament
Supplement Series 133

Published by JSOT Press
JSOT Press is an imprint of
Sheffield Academic Press Ltd
343 Fulwood Road
Sheffield S10 3BP
England

Typeset by Sheffield Academic Press
and
Printed on acid-free paper in Great Britain
by Biddles Ltd
Guildford

British Library Cataloguing in Publication Data

Syrén, Roger
    Forsaken First-Born: Study of a Recurrent
    Motif in the Patriarchal Narratives.—
    (JSOT Supplement Series, ISSN 0309-0787;
    No. 133)
    I. Title II. Series

    ISBN 1-85075-342-3

CONTENTS

PREFACE

The original manuscript to this book came about within the context of a larger project called 'The Outsider in the Old Testament', headed by Professor Karl-Johan Illman of Åbo Academy University, and sponsored by the Finnish Academy. While the project focused mainly on anonymous groups like children, orphans, widows, slaves and the poor, I chose to study named individuals, the first-born of the Patriarchs.

I thank Professor Illman for his willingness to include my study in his project. My manuscript subsequently underwent revision and edition for publication, and I extend my sincere thanks especially to Richard Davie and J. Webb Mealy at Sheffield Academic Press for their work in preparing my manuscript for publication.

I also thank my family, Marianne and the children, for an astoundingly tolerant attitude, so frequently tested!

For the biblical quotations I use *The Revised Standard Version*—if a quotation deviates from it, the translation will be my own.

Roger Syrén
November 1992

ABBREVIATIONS

AB	The Anchor Bible
AnBib	*Analecta Biblica*
ANET	*Ancient Near Eastern Texts*
AnOr	Analecta orientalia
ATD	Das Alte Testament Deutsch
BASOR	*Bulletin of the American Schools of Oriental Research*
BBB	Bonner Biblische Beiträge
BHS	*Biblia Hebraica Stuttgartensia*
Bib	*Biblica*
BKAT	Biblischer Kommentar: Altes Testament
BWANT	Beiträge zur Wissenschaft vom Alten und Neuen Testament
BZAW	Beihefte zur *Zeitschrift für die alttestamentliche Wissenschaft*
CAD	*The Assyrian Dictionary of the Oriental Institute of the University of Chicago*
CBC	Cambridge Bible Commentary
CBQ	*Catholic Biblical Quarterly*
EncJud	*Encyclopedia Judaica*
HAT	Handbuch zum Alten Testament
HSM	Harvard Semitic Monographs
HUCA	*Hebrew Union College Annual*
ICC	International Critical Commentary
IEJ	*Israel Exploration Journal*
JBL	*Journal of Biblical Literature*
JJS	*Journal of Jewish Studies*
JSOT	*Journal for the Study of the Old Testament*
JSOTSup	*Journal for the Study of the Old Testament*, Supplement Series
JTS	*Journal of Theological Studies*
Judaica	*Judaica: Beiträge zum Verständnis. . .*
KAT	Kommentar zum Alten Testament
NCB	New Century Bible
NEB	New English Bible
OrAnt	*Oriens Antiquus*
OTM	Old Testament Message
OTS	*Oudtestamentische Studiën*
RAC	*Reallexikon für Antike und Christentum*
RSV	Revised Standard Version

SJOT	*Scandinavian Journal of the Old Testament*
SNTSMS	Society for New Testament Studies Monograph Series
TBü	*Theologische Bücherei*
ThWAT	G.J. Botterweck and H. Ringgren (eds.), *Theologisches Wörterbuch zum Alten Testament*
TLZ	*Theologische Literatureitung*
TZ	*Theologische Zeitschrift*
WMANT	Wissenschaftliche Monographien zum Alten und Neuen Testament
ZAW	*Zeitschrift für die alttestamentliche Wissenschaft*
ZTK	*Zeitschrift für Theologie und Kirche*

INTRODUCTION

> The first-born very often seem to be losers in Genesis by the very condition of their birth.[1]

The purpose of this book is to examine the phenomenon of the 'forsaken first-born' in the book of Genesis. By this I mean the way in which the dignity of the first-born sons of Abraham, Isaac, Jacob and Joseph—Ishmael, Esau, Reuben and Manasseh—is disregarded, and the rights inherent in their status are taken from them and conferred on a younger brother. One might easily compare this with the motif in many folk tales of the youngest son outdoing his elder brothers in cleverness and skill. But unlike the folklore motif, in the book of Genesis the younger brother's success is not because of any courageous deed or heroic feat on his own part (Jacob may be clever, but he also cheats!). Instead, in three out of the four cases, the displacement of the elder by the younger is the result of somebody else's initiative and achievement.

With regard to literature, 'motif' is defined by *The Shorter Oxford Dictionary* (1970) as 'a distinctive feature or element of a design or composition; a particular type of subject; also, the dominant idea of a work'; and it is more generally defined by *The Random House Dictionary of the English Language* (1983) as 'a recurring subject, theme, idea, etc., esp. in a literary, artistic, or musical work'. The motif of the 'forsaken first-born' can hardly be said to be a 'distinctive' feature of the *literary composition* of Genesis as a whole. It is not a leading theme in Genesis in the sense that recognizing it is decisive for grasping the idea behind the composition of the book. Rather, it is confined to a more limited complex, namely the patriarchal narratives, where its occurrences are curiously regular.

However, Genesis is remarkably silent about the significance of the motif, and, in striking contrast to other motifs from Israel's history

---

1. R. Alter, *The Art of Biblical Narrative* (London: Allen & Unwin, 1981), p. 6.

(such as the Exodus, Sinai, and Israel as Yahweh's first-born or adopted son), it receives no attention in other parts of the Bible. For example, when the Psalmist entreats God to remember and punish the Edomites in Ps. 137.7, the plea is not undergirded by referring to Esau's loss of status, but by recalling Edom's aggression against Jerusalem during the turmoils leading up to the exile. Similarly, the reasons given by the prophets for Edom's punishment and destruction (e.g. Jer. 49.7-10; Ezek. 25.12-14; 35; Obadiah) refer to the violence against Judah—'for the murderous violence done to your brother Jacob' (Obad. 10). Allegations of 'murderous violence' are not substantiated in the biblical Esau–Jacob report, but are the product of the enmity between two peoples in the historical sphere. Nor is any appeal made to the portrayal of their personal antecedents in Genesis to back up the declamation in Mal. 1.2: 'I have loved Jacob, but I have hated Esau'. This impassioned statement follows a concatenation of recent historical events, and is not a paradigmatic application of the motif of the forsaken first-born. In Ps. 83.7-12 the Edomites and Ishmaelites keep company with the Moabites, Ammonites and others in gathering together against Israel and conspiring to bring about its downfall. Again, it is to history that the Psalmist turns, recollecting earlier failures by Israel's enemies (vv. 10-13) and summoning God to let their plans founder once more. But nothing is said to revive the memory of how Ishmael and Esau once had to step aside for Isaac and Jacob, although such a reminder would be most appropriate in this particular context. Only in St Paul does Abraham's expulsion of Ishmael and Hagar acquire a paradigmatic function, albeit by means of an allegorical adaptation.

Since the framework I am considering here is that of 'a literary work', my foremost task is a *literary analysis* of the texts in which the motif appears. This task applies to those texts which involve the respective first-born in person. I shall treat these texts in two ways: on the one hand working from the standpoint of traditional criticism; on the other being open to the *modus operandi* of modern 'literary approaches'[1] that treat biblical narrative as an art form operating according to rules intrinsically its own. Later I shall make some further statements concerning the usefulness of this approach compared

---

1. On this rather unhelpful term, cf. M. Sternberg, *The Poetics of Biblical Narrative: Ideological Literature and the Drama of Reading* (Indiana Literary Biblical Series; Bloomington: Indiana University Press, 1985), pp. 3-5.

to the historical methods. It will suffice here to say that in this study I will tolerate both 'old' and 'new'. This means that I will work on the texts in their present shape, dividing up each passage into sections appropriate to its own particular structure. This is not done primarily to lay bare any narrative strategy on the part of a biblical author, but to trace the essence of the motif in each of its individual presentations.

Problems of *historical origin and significance* will inevitably have to be addressed in this process, and so will questions pertaining to the *theology* behind the texts encountered. It is also important to trace the impact of the motif over a longer time-scale in later texts—however unyielding in this respect such texts may at first seem. The historical dimension of the motif will receive due attention insofar as its 'meaning' necessarily implies questions about its 'milieu', and conclusions will have to be drawn concerning the historical location of the texts. Other historical problems (such as the existence of 'Ishmaelite' tribes) will, however, be left for consideration in footnotes only. Finally, the essay will turn to a discussion of the *relevance* of the motif in its various textual and historical contexts.

Chapter 1

THE ISHMAEL TEXTS

The texts involving Ishmael are: Gen. 16.7-16; 17.15-27; 21.9-21; 25.9, 12-18. The texts cover Ishmael's life from his birth (ch. 16) to his death (25.17) and his descendants (25.13-16). Gen. 16.1-6 reports the conflict between Sarai and Hagar,[1] and Hagar's flight into the desert. The story moves on in vv. 7-14 to deal with the announcement of the birth of Ishmael (11), and vv. 15-16 narrates the birth. Gen. 17.1-4 proclaims the covenant between Abraham and Yahweh. As the visible mark of this covenant, the circumcision of every male is introduced. In vv. 23-27 Abraham performs the operation on all his household, Ishmael included—in fact, he is not only included, but circumcised first among the males of Abraham's family! Between vv. 14 and 23 is set another annunciation of a child's birth, this time the birth of Isaac to Sarai, renamed Sarah. This passage juxtaposes Ishmael and Isaac, as the lesser to the greater, with Isaac receiving the lion's share:

> As for Ishmael, I have heard you; behold, I will bless him. But I will establish my covenant with Isaac, whom Sarah shall bear to you at this season next year (Gen. 17.20-22).

The sections which interest me here are those directly involving Ishmael: 16.7-14, 17.15-21, 17.23-27 and 21.(8)9-21. In 16.7-14, my attention will focus on the oracles in vv. 11-12 because of their peculiar form-critical character. In ch. 17 it is the theological standpoint and the attitude taken toward Ishmael which deserves attention. Verses 21.9-21 are important for wider information on Ishmael.

---

1.   J. Van Seters thinks that Sarai's childlessness—rather than her husband's—was the real issue in an 'original' version of the story; cf. 'The Problem of Childlessness in Near Eastern Law and the Patriarchs of Israel', *JBL* 87 (1968), pp. 401-408 (403). Against him, cf. E. Blum, *Die Komposition der Vätergeschichte* (WMANT, 57: Neukirchen–Vluyn: Neukirchener Verlag, 1971), p. 318.

The general consensus among scholars applying source-critical tools to these texts is that the bulk of ch. 16 beongs to J, P being responsible for the genealogical framework (vv. 1a, 3, 15-16).[1] In ch. 17, by contrast, P is at work 'in every line of the chapter'.[2] The Genesis 21 section is commonly (Westermann excepted) assigned to E.

Genesis 16.7-16

Structure and Content

Verses 7-16 tell the story of Ishmael's birth in the desert (7). His mother is a forlorn refugee (8), but she is not forgotten by God. His angel meets her and promises her numerous offspring (9-10). This. promise is given additional force by the proclamation of the birth to her of a son (11-12). In thankful reverence, Hagar names Yahweh as the 'God of seeing' (13)—which also serves as an explanation of the name given to the well (14). Finally, the birth of Ishmael is recorded (15-16).

Several narrative motifs common to other biblical passages appear in this novelette. One is the figure of the Messenger, the *mal'ak yhwh*.[3] Another is the location of the event by a 'well in the desert': *'ên hammayim bammidbār* (v. 7). This rather vague location (the additional identification of the well with 'the spring on the way to Shur' is not original)[4] is a narrative cliché. In the Bible, springs and

---

1.   Cf. C. Westermann, *Genesis 12–36* (BKAT, 1/2; Neukirchen–Vluyn: Neukirchener Verlag, 1974), pp. 282, 298; G. von Rad, *Das erste Buch Mose: Genesis übersetzt und erklärt* (ATD, 2/4; Göttingen: Vandenhoeck & Ruprecht, 9th edn, 1972), p. 152; J. Skinner, *A Critical and Exegetical Commentary on Genesis* (ICC; Edinburgh: T. & T. Clark, 1912), p. 285. R. Kilian (*Die vorpriesterlichen Abrahamsüberlieferungen literarkritisch und traditionsgeschichtlich untersucht* [BBB, 24; Bonn: Peter Hanstein, 1966], p. 83) thinks that at some point the J-section must also have ended in a mention of Ishmael's birth. Others deny the influence of P proper in the chapter; cf. Blum, *Vätergeschichte*, pp. 315-16 (he does, however, recognize v. 16 as the result of a priestly revision).

2.   So Skinner, *Genesis*, p. 289. Cf. also Westermann, *Genesis 12–36*, p. 308; von Rad, *Genesis*, p. 154.

3.   For a closer treatment of this figure and a comparison with other Old Testament passages, cf. Westermann, *Genesis 12–36*, pp. 289-90.

4.   Cf. H. Gunkel, *Genesis übersetzt und erklärt* (Göttinger Handkommentar zum Alten Testament; Göttingen: Vandenhoeck & Ruprecht, 5th edn, 1922), p. 186; Westermann, *Genesis 12–36*, p. 291; Kilian, *Abrahamsüberlieferungen*, p. 76.

wells appear in a variety of contexts where they either act as venues for important confrontations and consultations or are used symbolically to represent fertility and life-giving power.[1] Wells also have a history as holy places inhabited by spirits and demons.[2] A well or the vicinity of a well, therefore, is a most appropriate place for an artful storyteller to stage a rendezvous between a god and a human.[3] Here, although the well serves as the location for an important rendezvous, a theophany,[4] it is not the well but the characters and the exchanges between them that are important.[5]

It is interesting to contrast this story with the second Hagar-in-the-desert story in ch. 21 (often, as mentioned above, ascribed to E, but by Westermann to a redactor [*Ergänzer*]).[6] In the latter story it is only because God lets his mother discover a life-saving 'well of water' that Ishmael is able to survive. In ch. 16, on the other hand, Hagar does not suffer thirst, and water does not figure in the story at all.

The other significant parts in the story are the oracles (vv. 11-12) and the dialogue between the *mal'āk* and Hagar, into which the oracles are inserted. It is this dialogue that provides the connecting link between vv. 7-14 and the beginning of the chapter. Appropriately, it

---

1. Waters and wells may also typify the assets of the promised land. Cf. J. Schreiner, עֵיִן '*ajin*, מַעְיָן *ma'jān*', *ThWAT*, VI, cols. 48-56 (53).

2. There is a wealth of literature on this topic; cf. P. Reymond, *L'eau, sa vie, et sa signification dans l'Ancien Testament* (VTSup, 6; Leiden: Brill, 1958), pp. 208-10, and more generally, W. Robertson Smith, *Lectures on the Religion of the Semites: The Fundamental Institutions* (ed. S.A. Cook; London: A. & C. Black, 3rd edn, 1927), pp. 135-37.

3. Cf. the religio-historical approach taken by Gunkel and several others following him to vv. 7 and 3-14. The deity appears in the story as the numen of the well (Gunkel, *Genesis*, pp. 187-88). Cf. also G. Heintz, 'בְּאֵר', *ThWAT*, I, cols. 500-503 (502) and the works mentioned in the previous note.

4. It thus plays a role similar to the ford of Jabbok in Gen. 32 or the mountain and the burning bush in Exod. 31 (note incidentally that, as here, the location is named).

5. Cf. J. Van Seters, *Abraham in History and Tradition* (New Haven: Yale University Press, 1975), p. 193. The well motif is shared with the betrothal scenes in Genesis. Alter (*The Art*, pp. 31-40) gives a detailed description of this 'type scene'. Another trait in common with betrothal scenes is the appearance of a woman; although here she plays the role not of the wife-to-be, but of a mother-to-be. The Ishmael story, probably, combines element from two genres: the betrothal scene and the theophany.

6. Cf. Westermann, *Genesis 12–36*, p. 414.

opens in v. 8, with the angel addressing Hagar as 'maid of Sarai'. Thus, Hagar's position in the family of Abram is emphasized, and the connection with the immediately preceding context is established. This connection is important for understanding the following conversation—without which it would seem rather pointless:

> 'Where do you come from?'
> 'From Sarai.'
> 'Go back to her'! (vv. 8-9).[1]

The second section of the dialogue begins at v. 10, and it too is attached to the opening section, though rather loosely. The dialogue is virtually introduced afresh: 'And the Angel of Yahweh said to her...' Verse 10 refers back to the promise given to Abraham in 13.16:

> I will make your descendants as the dust of the earth; so that if one can count the dust of the earth, your descendants also can be counted.

Gen. 16.10 conveys exactly the same message, only in negative form (although the verb for 'count' here is *spr* compared with *mnh* in 13.16):

> I will so greatly multiply your descendants that they cannot be numbered for multitude.

Thus Ishmael is, in effect, integrated into Abraham's family and is seen to share in the promise made to the patriarch.[2]

The dialogue then turns into a monologue, introduced again by the formula: 'And the Angel of Yahweh said...' This is followed by the annunciation of Ishmael's birth and a sketch of his character as a man who will dwell alone. The last section of the passage, vv. 13-14, contains Hagar's reaction to the angel's message, a reaction which expresses itself in the naming of the deity (13) and the well (14). This renaming, as can be seen in, for example, the stories of Abraham and Jacob, is another biblical convention[3] both answering the need to

---

1. On vv. 8-15, cf. Van Seters, *Abraham*, p. 194.
2. Westermann (*Genesis 12–36*, pp. 292-93) gives a different interpretation of v. 9, and he explains v. 10 as a late addition describing Abraham as the father of many nations following the pattern: *promise of a son–promise of many descendants*. Cf. also Blum, *Vätergeschichte*, p. 317 ('a late expansion').
3. Westermann (*Genesis 12–36*, p. 295) refers especially to Gen. 22.

express the hero/heroine's deeply felt gratitude and embroidering the story with a popular etymology.[1]

The structure of 16.7-14 may be summarized as follows:

A   The Lord's Angel appearing by the well (7)
B   Dialogue and proclamation (8-12)
   1. Dialogue between the Angel and Hagar (8-9)
      a. Question and answer (8, introductory formula 1, *wymr*)
      b. Command—following from the answer (9, introductory
         formula 2)
   2. The message (10-12)
      a. Promise of many descendants (10, introductory formula 3)
      b. Promise of a son—the Annunciation (12, introductory
         formula 4)
C   Hagar's reaction: the namegiving (13)
D   The name of the well (14)

B is a patchwork of formally if not logically disconnected elements; nevertheless, the links between them (*wymr...*) are still clearly visible.[2] On the other hand, B provides the main thrust of the passage to which A is only the prelude. D is obviously meant to supplement v. 7 with a more exact identification of the place. *'al-kēn* joins C and D together.

The framework of the passage seems to have been borrowed from a theophany story, augmented with later material and adjusted to the context. I do not share Van Seters's view that 16.1-12 is one original unit exhibiting all the prerequities of a folktale (according to Olrik's 'epic laws' of folklore).[3]

1.   On the place-name, cf. Westermann, *Genesis 12–36*, pp. 297-98; Kilian (*Abrahamsüberlieferungen*, pp. 82-83) considers other possible interpretations of the text. Cf. also H. Schmid, 'Ismael in Alten Testament und im Koran', *Judaica* 32 (1976), pp. 76-81, 119-29 (77).

2.   Skinner (*Genesis*, p. 287) thinks vv. 9-10 are a double interpolation; v. 10 he considers as 'made up of phrases characteristic of redactional additions to JE'. Similarly also Gunkel, *Genesis*, p. 184. Cf. also Kilian, *Abrahamsüberlieferungen*, p. 76 (for the whole chapter, cf. pp. 74-75).

3.   Cf. Van Seters, *Abraham*, pp. 194-96. He includes vv. 1 and 3 in the original tale and plays down the influence of P. The roots of the passage lie in a pre-Yahwistic 'written level of the tradition' (p. 311).

Verses 11-12. Verses 11-12[1] contain the proclamation to Hagar of the birth of Ishmael, accompanied by a brief sketch of his character and destiny. In its present context as part of the longer Hagar story (beginning at v. 7), v. 11 forms the climax. The annunciation of Ishmael's birth uses the same words as many others in the Old Testament: Samson (Judg. 13.3); Immanuel (Isa. 7.14);[2] Josiah (1 Kgs 13.2) and Solomon (1 Chron. 22.9). The annunciation-formula can be divided into a number of smaller sections,[3] one of the most important being v. 12, in which the child's future achievements are foretold.[4] However, although the two verses belong together in this context, they are hardly to be regarded as an original unit. On the contrary, v. 12 can be taken as originally independent and subsequently incorporated into the formula. This too is in agreement with Westermann.[5] Its *Gattung* is clearly 'the tribal oracle' (*Stammesspruch*). It forms a tricolon whose middle part contains a neat chiastic parallelism between 'his hand on every man' and 'every man's hand on him'. By far the closest parallels to this verse are the animal metaphors in Genesis 49:[6]

1.   For textual details, cf. Kilian, *Abrahamsüberlieferungen*, pp. 78-79, 84-87. In Kilian's traditio-historical view, vv. 11-14 constitutes the oldest section of ch. 16, probably rooted in an Ishmaelitic tradition.

2.   On Isa. 7.14, see A. Laato, *Who is Immanuel? The Rise and Foundering of Isaiah's Messianic Expectations* (Åbo: Åbo Academy Press, 1988), pp. 130-31.

3.   For a formal analysis of the *Gattung*, cf. Van Seters, *Abraham*, pp. 194-95. He finds the explanation of the name in 11c to be an addition. Cf. also Westermann, *Genesis 12–36*, pp. 293-94. The constant element in all these texts, as Westermann points out, is the annunciation itself: 'You will conceive and bear a son. . . ' But a possible exception to this might be 2 Sam. 7.12-13 (on Solomon), where v. 13 shows a strong similarity with 1 Chron. 22.10 as the follow-up verse to the annunciation in v. 9. In which case 2 Sam. 7.12, spoken to David, could well be regarded as a modified annunciation.

4.   Corresponding to Westermann's fourth section; cf. *Genesis 12–36*, p. 293.

5.   Cf. *Genesis 12–36*, p. 295.

6.   Cf. also the passages referred to by Westermann, *Genesis 12–36*, p. 294; he does not elaborate on the parallel to Gen. 49. For some brief notes on the form of the Stammesspruch, cf. also *idem*, *Genesis 37–50* (BKAT, 1/3; Neukirchen–Vluyn: Neukirchener Verlag, 1982), pp. 250-51. A.H.J. Gunneweg ('Über den Sitz im Leben der sog. Stammessprüche [Gen. 49, Deut. 33, Jud. 5]', *ZAW* 76 [1964], pp. 245-55 [248, 250]) sees the animal comparison and the wordplay as the two basic elements of the tribal saying. Strictly speaking, the animal comparison is an identification, not a mere comparison. The two forms would also constitute the oldest form of the tribal sayings, serving as the self-description of the tribe at the tribal assembly

vv. 9 (on Judah), 14 (Issachar), 17 (Dan), 21 (Naphtali) and 27 (Benjamin). Each stich of Gen. 16.12 contains a separate statement; in other words, there is no parallelism between the lines. On the basis of Gen. 16.12, the individual elements of a *Stammesspruch* can be broadly characterized as follows:

A   The metaphor: so-and-so (the pronoun 'he'; the name in Gen. 49) is (like) such-and-such.
B   A concise phrase characterizing the hero as belligerent or valiant.
C   A comment indicating residence (verbs like *škn*, 'dwell', or *rbṣ*, 'rest', and so on.

The distinctive elements at least partially correspond to the structure of the sayings in Genesis 49:

v. 9   A   Judah is a lion's whelp
        B   from the prey, my son, you have gone up
        C   He couched, he rested (*rbṣ*) like a lion[1]

v. 14   A   Issachar is a gelded ass
        B   —
        C   crouching (*rbṣ*) between the sheepfolds

v. 17   A   Dan shall be a viper on the road (a snake on the path)
        B   who bites the horse's fetlock so that the rider tumbles
            backwards
        C   —

v. 21   A   (?) Naphtali is a hind let loose
        B   (?) giving beautiful words

v. 27   A   Benjamin is a ravening wolf
        B   in the morning he devours the prey (in the evening he
            snatches a share of the spoil)
        C   —

In these verses, the metaphoric language of A continues into B and C:[2] the biting snake, the lion and the wolf taking prey. By contrast, in

(*Amphiktyonie*). This is no longer a tenable position, but Gunneweg's organization of the material is still fully valid. F.M. Cross ('Reuben, First-Born of Jacob', *ZAW* 100 [1988], pp. 44-65 [49]) argues along similar lines for a *Sitz im Leben* for 'the blessings' at pilgrimage festivals or assemblies for holy war. The cycle of the blessings is the primary *Gattung*; the individual blessing did not develop independently. This may hold true for Gen. 49, but what of an isolated saying on Ishmael?
  1.   Cf. also Num. 24.9: 'He couched, he lay down (*škb*) like a lion. . . '
  2.   Cf. Westermann, *Genesis 37–50*, pp. 260.

16.12 B abandons the metaphor and gives the interpretation, referring to the human hero directly. Despite this, the significance of B is similar in all these cases: it is not a nomadic life-style that is implied but the need for a tribe to defend or expand its territorial claims. This fits well with the point made by Westermann,[1] that Gen. 49.27 and Deut. 33.12 demonstrate two different stages of a tribe's settlement: the former one of robbery and struggle for survival and land, the latter one of 'dwelling in security'.

As seen from the above examples, the three elements A, B and C do not necessarily always appear together. For obvious reasons A is the constant, but B or C may be missing or expanded. Only in 49.9 do all three appear together as in 16.12. In 49.14 B is missing, and in 49.21 what I have marked as B seems devoid of any warlike meaning. C is missing in 49.17, 21 and 27. This suggests that when all the elements A, B and C appear together they form a more complete (and possibly more original) version of the metaphorical *Stammesspruch* than when either B or C is missing.[2] Nor do all three elements necessarily occur together when an animal metaphor is not employed, as in vv. 20 and 22. Another variation of the *Stammesspruch* is the appearance of a wordplay on the ancestor's name instead of a metaphor, as in the case of Dan and Gad in Genesis 49 and Japheth in 9.27. Moreover, in the latter instance a C element appears in the middle:

> May God enlarge (*ypt*) Japheth, and let him dwell in the tents of Shem, and may Canaan be his slave![3] (Gen. 9.27).

In its present state, the animal metaphor, and indeed the whole passage 16.7-14, reveals a favourable, or at least neutral, attitude towards Ishmael on the part of the biblical writer and/or sources.[4] Elsewhere in the Bible the wild ass is the typical unfettered wild animal, alone

---

1. Cf. Westermann, *Genesis 37–50*, p. 275.

2. This structure seems only to appear in Genesis. In Deut. 33 the sayings are completely transformed, appearing as the blessings of Moses; see Westermann, *Genesis 37–50*, p. 250.

3. Cf. also C. Westermann, *Genesis 1–11* (BKAT, 1/1; Neukirchen–Vluyn: Neukirchener Verlag, 1974), pp. 655-66.

4. As D.J. Zucker ('Conflicting Conclusions: The Hatred of Isaac and Ishmael', *Judaism* 39 [1990], pp. 37-46 [45]) points out, there is a significant disparity between the 'neutral' attitude of the Bible and that in the rabbinic sources. Cf. also M. Ohana, 'La polémique judéo–islamique et l'image d'Ismaël dans Targum Pseudo-Jonathan et dans Pirke de Rabbi Eliezer', *Augustinianum* 15 (1975), pp. 367-87 (368).

and free to go its own way (Hos. 8.9; Job 39.5).[1] Its true home is in
the desert (Jer. 2.24; Job 24.5), where God provides it with food and
drink (Job 6.5; Ps. 104.11), but when there is drought it starves like
other creatures (Jer. 14.6). In Hos. 8.9 and Jer. 2.24 the animal serves
as an illustration of Israel's apostasy: as the wild ass in her heat
exposes herself to her mates, Israel lustfully submits itself to foreign
gods. Apart from this, nothing pejorative is associated with the wild
ass—and in this instance it symbolizes Israel and not her seducers.

Like the wild ass, Ishmael is predestined to a solitary, wandering
life. In this respect he can be compared to Cain, although, unlike Cain,
the biblical narrator does not impute any crime or guilt to Ishmael.
Yet despite this, the prospects for Ishmael's life are not unlike Cain's:
both are sent away from their own family and community (Gen. 4.14).

Gen. 16.12 may not originally have been connected with Ishmael. It
is an anonymous saying; the opening 'he' is determined more by form
than content and could refer to anyone.[2] However, when the wild ass
metaphor is applied to Ishmael, he can be seen primarily as the per-
sonification of desert-dwellers who are in constant interaction with
other groups ('his hand on every man') without anything specific
being implied about the individual himself.[3]

The last line, *w'l pny kl 'hyw yškn*, has been interpreted in various
ways. I have taken it to mean 'he shall dwell opposite his brethren',
but compare the NEB: 'he shall live at odds with all his kinsmen'. *'l
pny* has a very wide range of meanings: 'in the face of'; 'before';
'opposite to'; 'against'; 'to the cost of'; 'to the east of'. The RSV and
NEB favour 'to the east of' in cases where a place-name follows—see,
for example, Gen. 23.19; 25.9; 50.13; Exod. 16.14; Josh. 13.3; 17–19
(several instances); 1 Chron. 5.10. Davidson and Speiser[4] argue for a
hostile meaning: 'in defiance of'. Gunkel, von Rad and Westermann
are, on balance, more neutral.[5]

---

1. Cf. S. Bar-Efrat, *Narrative Art in the Bible* (JSOTSup, 70; Sheffield: JSOT
Press, 1989), p. 207.
2. Cf. Kilian, *Abrahamsüberlieferungen*, p. 79.
3. In view of such biblical passages as Gen. 37.25 and 1 Chron. 27.30, one
might sooner expect the camel (admittedly not a 'wild' animal) to be Ishmael's 'totem'.
4. R. Davidson, *Genesis 12–50* (CBC; London: Cambridge University Press,
1979), p. 53; E.A. Speiser, *Genesis: Introduction, Translation, and Notes* (AB; New
York: Doubleday, 1964), p. 118.
5. Gunkel, *Genesis*, p. 188; von Rad, *Genesis*, p. 148; Westermann, *Genesis
12–36*, p. 278; cf. also Zucker, 'Conflicting Conclusions', p. 39, who takes it

A couple of formal parallel expressions should be noted: Lev. 10.3, *w'l pny kl h'm 'kbd* (NEB: 'in the presence of'), and Deut. 2.25, *'l pny h'mym* (NEB: 'upon'). However, the context and content of these verses cannot be compared directly with Gen. 16.12. A more closely related parallel is Gen. 25.18:

> They [the sons of Ishmael] dwelt from Havilah to Shur which is . . . (*'l pny*) Egypt on the way to Shur; he settled [for *npl*?] . . . (*'l pny*) all his brothers.

The reference to Ishmael and 'all his brothers' in the second half of this sentence compares very closely with Gen. 16.12. Only the verb is different: in 25.18 it is *npl*, literally 'fall' (RSV, NEB: 'settled'). Gen. 25.18b may then be taken to be either an independent variant of 16.12 (so Westermann),[1] or perhaps a secondary comment upon 16.12. The latter seems more probable; a redactor may have found reason to say of Ishmael's sons in a slightly varied form what had earlier been said of their father—like father like son![2]

In Gen. 25.18 *'l pny* occurs twice, and its meaning may be the same both times; compare the RSV—'opposite Egypt' and 'over against all his people'—with the NEB—'east of Egypt' and 'to the east of his brothers'. The meaning is certainly not the same as in 50.1, where *npl* together with *'l pny* has a more literal meaning: 'Joseph fell on his father's face (and wept over him and kissed him)'. As seen above, the verb in 25.18 is usually translated 'settled' (Gunkel, von Rad, Westermann), indicating the area inhabited by Ishmael. This is supported by the occurrence of *nplym* in Judg. 7.12, referred to by Gunkel and Westermann,[3] and also by the use of *npl* in the expression *npl l- bn ḥlh*, 'to fall to so-and-so for an inheritance', in Num. 34.2 and Judg. 18.1, referring to the territorial boundaries of the Israelite tribes.

Gen. 16.12 and 25.18 can be taken, then, either to imply hostility between related tribes, or merely as a broad indication of the area the Ishmaelites inhabited—it may even imply that Ishmael did not possess any territory distinctly his own. I would opt for the latter interpreta-

---

to suggest friendship: 'alongside all his kinsmen'!

1. Westermann, *Genesis 12–36*, p. 488.

2. Cf. Gunkel's view that 25.18 was based on 16.12 as its fulfilment (*Genesis*, p. 190).

3. Gunkel, *Genesis*, p. 190; Westermann, *Genesis 12–36*, p. 278; Skinner, *Genesis*, p. 354.

tion ('opposite'), because of the phrase 'all his brothers/kinsmen'. Defining Ishmael's area of habitation as being 'opposite his brothers' is a convenient way of distancing him from these 'brothers' without making explicit the nature of the relationship between them. The plural 'all his brothers/kinsmen' contradicts the context of 16.7-16[1] (in Gen. 16–17 and 21 as a whole, Ishmael is contrasted with Isaac alone). But again the *Gattung* of the *Stammesspruch* has to be considered.

In Genesis 49, the 'brothers' are twice referred to, in order to distance and distinguish the individual ancestor from the rest:

49.8   Judah, your brothers shall praise you;
. . .
your father's sons shall bow down before you
(*yšhthww lk bny 'byk*);

49.26   . . . may [the blessings] be on the head of Joseph, and on the brow of him who was separate from [or: prince among][2] his brothers (compare also Deut. 33.16).

Isaac's blessing of Jacob in Gen. 27.29 also shows a similar use of 'brothers' as an epithet:

Let peoples serve you
and nations bow down to you.
Be lord over your brothers
and may your mothers' sons bow down
before you . . . (*wyšthww lk bny 'mk*).

(Compare this with v. 37, 'All his brothers I have given to him for servants'.) No more than in Gen. 16.12 does 'brothers' here fit the immediate context. In all three sayings, the 'brothers' constitute the group from which the hero is distinguished.[3] This also applies to 25.18.[4]

1.   Attempts to justify 'brothers' from the context of the Isaac/Ishmael sections seem somewhat forced, e.g. H. Schmid's proposal to understand 'brothers' as 'half-brothers' or Isaac and his folks ('Ismael', pp. 78-79).
2.   On *nzyr 'hyw*, cf. R. Syrén, *The Blessings in the Targums: A Study on the Targumic Interpretations of Genesis 49 and Deuteronomy 33* (Acta Academiae Aboensis, 64/1; Åbo: Åbo Akademi, 1986), pp. 60-61.
3.   This formal aspect on the tribal saying and its offshoots is totally missed by S.H. Blank, 'Studies in Post-Exilic Universalism', *HUCA* 11 (1938), pp. 159-91 (180). He thinks that the referrence to 'brothers' in the plural is an error: 'It must be either that this blessing is the reflection of a variant tradition which knew of other sons of Rebekah, or, as we believe, that it expresses a vague hope that renascent Judah shall gain the position of leadership among related groups. . .'

As Isaac's blessing of Jacob indicates, the use of the plural 'brothers' in these passages does not necessarily fit the immediate context—Jacob, too, like Ishmael, had but one brother. Westermann[1] understands the reference primarily to reflect rivalries between different tribal groups. But it is also clearly some form of appellation, fixed by long tradition, which gives the hero a distinctive identity of his own. An identity is always acquired in relationship to and in confrontation with others. This holds true especially for the biblical portrayal of Ishmael, whose identity seems to be conferred upon him by others. He remains an indistinct and passive figure. Throughout he is the object of other people's actions, and he is never allowed to speak for himself. (In 21.17 God is said to have heard 'the voice' of Ishmael in the desert, but the MT would have to be emended from 'she' to 'he' before it was certain that 'the voice' was that of Ishmael.) Gen. 16.12 must be interpreted in line with this: the 'brothers' of Ishmael are in reality the creators of his personality.

The Significance of 16.7-16 for the Biblical Portrayal of Ishmael
Von Rad observes that in 16.9-16 not a word is uttered about the great promise to Abraham. This is hardly the case for v. 10, which, as I have shown above, refers to Gen. 13.16 (cf. also 15.5).[2] But von Rad's observation is correct as far as vv. 11-12 is concerned. But then an allusion to the promise given to Abraham is hardly to be expected, at least not in v. 12. Here the context is not the fulfilment of God's promises to Abraham, but the integration of the whole of Israel into one nation. And in this process it would have been clear that Ishmael was an outsider who had to remain *'l pny* his 'brothers'. In historical terms this would allow for Westermann's dating[3] of v. 12 to a time

4.   In the curse of Canaan, Gen. 9.25, already referred to above, the phrase 'his brothers' is evidently intended to distance him from Shem and Japheth—in this case, the 'brothers' of the immediate context. They are his masters, he their slave. Cf. von Rad, *Genesis*, p. 103.

1.   *Genesis 12–36*, pp. 537-38.

2.   Cf. also Westermann, *Genesis 12–36*, p. 293, who discerns in v. 11 a late interpolation to include Hagar and the offspring of Ishmael among the peoples stemming from Abraham.

3.   *Genesis 12–36*, p. 295. For attempts to locate the Ishmaelites chronologically and geographically, cf. J. Van Seters, *Abraham*, pp. 37, 63. Cf. also E. Meyer, *Die Israeliten und ihre Nachbarstämme: Alttestamentliche Untersuchungen* (Halle: Max Niemeyer, 1906), pp. 3-22. Blum (*Vätergeschichte*, p. 341 n. 3) would prefer to

after the settlement in Canaan when settlers and nomadic groups were
competitors as well as, at times, allies. The biblical sources (e.g. Gen.
25) suggest that certain groups enjoyed a closer relationship with the
Israelite tribes than others.[1] Biblical historiography explained this
relationship in terms of Ishmael's origin and destiny: he was born a

link the Ishmael of Gen. 16.12 with a specific tribal group, but concedes that such a
group is absent from the historical record. The list in 25.12-17 of Ishmael's sons
would, in Blum's mind, point more generally to North Arabic tribes. I. Eph'al (*The
Ancient Arabs: Nomads on the Borders of the Fertile Crescent 9th–5th Centuries BC*
[Jerusalem: Magnes, 2nd edn, 1984], p. 236) supposes that since the Midianites and
Amalekites were identified with the Ishmaelites (cf. the following note) the latter
would at one time have been a leading confederation of nomads in southern
Palestine, and their name would occasionally have been attached to other groups.
This comes close to my own view: 'Ishmaelites' in the Old Testament, although
formally a gentilic adjective, may not refer to any identifiable tribe at all. It is important to note that the Assyrian sources do not mention any ethnic group by the name of
Ishmael (cf. Eph'al, *The Ancient Arabs*, pp. 166-68). In the Old Testament the term
may imply socio-economically distinct, rather than racially related groups. So it
seems when it appears in Gen. 37.25 and 1 Chron. 27.30 referring to tradesmen and
camel-breeders. In the latter passage, the Chronicler states that an 'Ishmaelite' and a
'Hagrite' were officers at King David's court. While the other people on the list are
identified by the name of their father, or, alternatively, by a gentilic name indicating
where they came from, the term 'the Ishmaelite' for Obil (over the camels) and 'the
Hagrite' for Jaziz (over the small cattle) do not follow any such pattern. It is possible, therefore, that these terms were chosen because of the particular task assigned to
these persons. Along similar lines see E.A. Knauf, *Ismael: Untersuchungen zur
Geschichte Palästinas und Nordarabiens im 1. Jahrtausend v. Chr.* (Abhandlungen
des deutschen Palästinavereins; Wiesbaden: Otto Harrassowitz, 2nd edn, 1989),
pp. 13-14. Nowhere is Ishmael specified as the forefathers of the Ishmaelites. As far
as they can be identified, the names of his sons in Gen. 25.13-17 (1 Chron. 1.29-31;
cf. also Isa. 21.11-16) stand for places in the Syrian-Arabian desert; cf.
Westermann, *Genesis 12–36*, p. 487; Eph'al, *The Ancient Arabs*, pp. 236-37. This
is in stark contrast to the equation of Esau with Edom. Schmid ('Ismael', pp. 123-
24) defines the Ishmaelites of the Old Testament as desert dwellers and Bedouins,
and Knauf (*Ismael*, pp. 49, 113) defines them as a North Arabic confederation of
proto-Bedouins (on *Shumu'il*, cf. pp. 1, 45).

1.   The relationship of Israel suggested here with Ishmael's children is the
reverse of that with the arch-enemies, the Amalekites and the Philistines; although
this is in tension with Judg. 6, where the Amalekites join the Midianites against
Israel. The Midianites themselves are identified as 'Ishmaelites' by wearing special
insignia (8.24). This in turn contradicts Gen. 25.2, in which Midian is the son of
Abraham by Keturah. According to 1 Sam. 15.7 the Amalekites inhabited the same
area as the Ishmaelites in Gen. 25.18. Cf. also in Ps. 83.7.

son of Abraham, but was to be sent away to live apart from his father
and the rest of his family. Indeed, from his birth he is set apart; he is
born in the desert, far away from his father's house, and his mother
has to care for him on her own. This is in striking contrast[1] to Isaac,
who is born a free son, in his father's household. In addition to the
aetiolological motif emphasized by Blum,[2] the idea of Ishmael's separation from the house of Abraham is central to ch. 16.

The fact that both are named by Abraham—using identical wording; cf. Gen. 16.15, 21.3—does not detract from the contrast between
Ishmael's and Isaac's birth. The insertion of the naming into the birth
stories is intended to stress Abraham's paternal authority, not the
equal status of his two sons (name-giving in P is always performed by
the father). Moreover, 16.15 contradicts 16.11 (J), where Hagar is
instrumental in naming her offspring.[3]

Genesis 17

Structure and Content

Chapter 17 begins by restating the age of Abraham, thus connecting
the following event (Yahweh's revelation) with the end of ch. 16. It is
now 13 years later (17.25). The function of the chapter within the
larger unit beginning at ch. 15 is to repeat and confirm the promise
given in 15.5-7 (vv. 7-8). But the chapter also lays the theological foun-
dation for the promises and the covenant, materialized in circumcision.

The circumcision of Abraham's two sons means that the promise
has finally come true. A new element is introduced: the promises in
chs. 12 and 15 make no specific demands on Abraham (apart from the
commandment to leave Haran for Canaan, 12.1). But now God assigns
to Abraham and his descendants the task of upholding the covenant
from generation to generation by performing the rite of circumcision
on every male (9-14). Verse 14 sanctions the law of circumcision (in the
form of a curse) and prescribes the punishment for failure to observe
it. An uncircumcised male is to be cut off altogether from the people.

---

1.   Contrast is of course an essential part of the plot development in the Bible; cf.
Sternberg, *Poetics*, p. 366. On the effect of contrast from a sociological point of
view, cf. D.L. Smith, *The Religion of the Landless: The Social Context of the
Babylonian Exile* (Bloomington, IN: Meyer Stone, 1989), p. 56.

2.   *Vätergeschichte*, pp. 317-19.

3.   Westermann, *Genesis 12–36*, p. 298.

The chapter comprises three larger sections, which in turn can be divided into smaller units:[1]

I	1-3a	Yahweh appears to Abram
II	3b-22	God's speeches
II.a	3b-14	God's first and second speeches
II.b	15-22	God's third and fourth speeches
III	23-27	Abraham carries out the circumcision in accordance with God's ordinance

The larger sections I-III begin with a main verb that indicates the character of the literary unit that follows:

I	*wyhy 'brm. . .wyr' yhwh*
II	*wydbr 'tw 'lhym l'mr*
III	*wyqḥ 'brm*

Section II is also separated from III by appending the very formal statement in v. 22: 'And when he had finished talking with him, God went up from Abraham'. The verb *wyr'* in v. 1 thus corresponds to the concluding verb *wy'l* in v. 22.

In telling contrast to ch. 16, in ch. 17 there is very little action.[2] The circumcision carried out in vv. 23-27 is the only thing that actually 'happens'. Instead, the stress lies on what God has to say to Abraham and what Abraham is told to do. Accordingly, God is the subject of most of the verbs appearing in the chapter.

The Unity of the Chapter
For a long time, scholarly opinion has unanimously held ch. 17 to be a work of the Priestly writer/source. In Westermann's words it is 'at the centre of the Priestly representation of the Patriarchal history'. But, he continues, the chapter is not a purely literary creation independent of any preceding tradition. On the contrary, P's theological reflections are a development of both oral and literary traditions that originated in the age of the Patriarchs themselves.[3]

---

1. Cf. also Westermann's division: *Genesis 12–36*, pp. 306-7; *idem*, Genesis 17 und die Bedeutung von *berit*', *TLZ* 101 (1976), cols. 161-70 (163).
2. Cf. Westermann, *Genesis 12–36*, p. 305; Gunkel, *Genesis*, p. 267; S. McEvenue, *The Narrative Style of the Priestly Writer* (AnBib, 50; Rome: Biblical Institute Press, 1971), pp. 149-50.
3. Its main thrust is actualization of the promises to the fathers; cf. Westermann, *Genesis 12–36*, p. 308 (the quotation above is my translation from the German edition).

A number of arguments in support of P authorship are given by
Gunkel,[1] although he also remarks that the descriptions in chs. 17 and
23 are lengthier than the short notices that predominate in P's
Abraham story. Among the sources used by P, McEvenue has pointed
to Genesis 15 and 18. He concludes that P remained faithful to the
sources, and that the changes made were for the purpose of theological
clarification and in order to reduce the narrative element (a characteristic feature of the entire P[g] creation).[2]

Although there is unanimity over the general authorship of P, there
is a wide variety of opinion concerning its precise components. The P-
source is commonly believed to incorporate a *Grundschrift* (P[g]),
accompanied by later additions and extensions (P[s]).[3] Opinions differ
on how to distinguish between P[g] and P[s] material, or even as to whether
different strands in the chapter exist at all. Elliger assigns the whole
chapter to the *Grundschrift*.[4]

Gunkel divides the chapter into two main sections: vv. 1-22 consists
of God's two speeches to which vv. 23-27 forms an appendix (actually
the first of two appendices; the second is to be found in 21.1b, 2b, 3,
4, 5). Whether or not the author of this appendix would have to be
identical with the one responsible for the first section is not clear;
Gunkel only points out that it presupposes and develops vv. 10-14.[5]

Westermann's division of the chapter is similar: vv. 23-27, the

1. Gunkel, *Genesis*, p. 264.
2. McEvenue, *Narrative Style*, pp. 149-54. He gives a detailed survey of the
material he suggests was extracted from chs. 15 and 18, and notes the changes in its
organization.
3. K. Elliger, 'Sinn und Ursprung der priesterlichen Geschichtserzählung',
ZTK 49 (1952), pp. 121-43 (121). See also J.G. Vink, 'The Date and Origin of the
Priestly Code in the Old Testament', *OTS* 15 (1969), pp. 1-144 (8-10). For a review
of opinions on the Priestly layer and the date of P, see Blum, *Vätergeschichte*,
pp. 446-50, who refuses to split the Priestly layer into separate strands or sources,
but uses the term 'the priestly stratum (*Schicht*)' for the redactional and traditio-
historical activities of the Priestly school. Whether one should talk of a 'source' or a
redactional 'reworking' within the Priestly school is not a question of decisive
importance for my argument on the following pages.
4. Cf. Elliger, 'Sinn und Ursprung', p. 121. Elliger's P[g] is a modification of
the earlier concept; he stresses that (1) only such material be assigned to P[g] as seems
to belong to it 'in an organic way', and (2) it has no continuation in Joshua. P[g] originated during the Exile in order to offer comfort to the Jews in Babylon; cf. pp. 122,
143.
5. Cf. Gunkel, *Genesis*, p. 272.

carrying out of the commandment, together with a genealogical note, forms the concluding section. Westermann thinks that the two main verbs in v. 23—'Abraham took' and 'he circumcised'—would be sufficient to show that the commandment was put into practice. Accordingly, the rest of section is an expansion giving more precise details on the practise of the circumcision rite. However, he does not give any details about the possibility of a different hand behind the concluding section.[1]

McEvenue gives an excellent review in his 'Table IV' of how scholars divide Genesis 17 into different strands.[2] He also examines the structure of ch. 17 (which he designates 'the oath to Abraham') and how it fits in with the overall framework and literary technique of P. The structure is found to be similar to that of Gen. 6.9-10 and 9.28-29. The whole pericope (1-25) is bound together in the form of a palistrophe (6 + 1 + 6). The chapter is made up of five speeches by God, with similar introductions, the third speech forming the centre enclosed by two sections: 1-8 and 15-25. The structure and style of ch. 17 are characterized by the development of a combination of sources (Gen. 15 and 18) from intention to fact and from vague to specific,[3] framed by vv. 1a, b and 22.24-27. Overall, McEvenue concludes that Genesis 17 shows no innovations in comparison with P's usual style (repetition, echo, exact detail, interlocking symmetry, palistrophe and panel-writing). However, it is different in that the chapter contains the least narrative out of the P-texts, and therefore shows no evident relationship to children's literature—McEvenue's favourite comparison. This is used to support his suggestion of a *Sitz im Leben* for P as a kind of catechesis. McEvenue's outline of the composition of the chapter is based on the belief that it constitutes one undivided whole. Any attempts to make the traditional distinctions between different sources are expressly rejected.[4]

The most interesting exchange of opinions on Genesis 17 from a

---

1. Westermann, *Genesis 12–36*, pp. 307, 326-27.
2. McEvenue, *Narrative Style*, p. 192. For a further review of opinions on the chapter, cf. S.R. Külling, *Zur Datierung der 'Genesis-P-Stücke' namentlich des Kapitels Genesis XVII* (Kampen: Kok, 1964), pp. 250-52.
3. McEvenue, *Narrative Style*, pp. 149-52; on the following, cf. pp. 160-83.
4. Cf. McEvenue, *Narrative Style*, p. 148 n. He is critical not least of von Rad's approach, concerning which see further below. Also Van Seters (*Abraham*, pp. 285, 287) defends the unity.

source-critical angle has come from von Rad's treatment of the chapter
in his *Die Priesterschrift im Hexateuch* (1934) and the ensuing reaction
from P. Humbert. Von Rad distinguishes two sources: P^A, vv. 15-22
(the covenant concerning Sarah and Isaac); and P^B, vv. 1-8; 9-14; 23-
27 (the covenant with Abraham and the circumcision). He takes P^A
and P^B to be doublets, based on two parallel traditions about God's
promises to Abraham. P^A is the older source—which, according to
von Rad, makes vv. 15-22 older than the rest of the chapter. One reason for this is its livelier and more picturesque character. Verses
23-27 represent a later recasting of the original report of how the circumcision was carried out. In addition he notes certain parallels and
repetitions, between, for example, vv. 6, 7 and 2, and between the
passages vv. 1-8 and vv. 15-22 (the latter passage being a parallel, not
a continuation of the former).[1]

Humbert[2] expresses both approval and criticism of von Rad's conclusions. Referring to Gunkel and Steuernagel,[3] Humbert supports the
separation of vv. 15-22 from 9-14. The two passages clearly disagree
on some crucial points, for example, the number of people affected by
the law of circumcision. Whereas 9-14 refers to Abraham and all his
descendants, including Ishmael, 15-22 restricts the covenant to Sarah,
Isaac and Isaac's descendants.[4] But Humbert reverses the relative
dating: 15-22 stem from a later hand than the rest of the chapter. The
passage originated not from a parallel source document, but as a later
addition to the original text of P. Humbert also disagrees with von
Rad concerning the parallel stories and repetitions—how could two
independent sources possibly contain such remarkable parallels?
Verses 6-7 do not repeat v. 2; rather, vv. 2-7 unfolds a clear and
progressive train of thought in the transition from intention to act.
Humbert's criticisms have led to some reconsiderations on von Rad's

1.   Cf. G. von Rad, *Die Priesterschrift im Hexateuch literarisch untersucht und theologisch gewertet* (BWANT, 65; Stuttgart: Kohlhammer, 1934), pp. 20-23. For ch. 17, von Rad follows M. Löhr, *Untersuchungen zum Hexateuchproblem. I. Der Priesterkodex in der Genesis* (BZAW, 38; Berlin: de Gruyter, 1924), p. 11.
2.   P. Humbert, 'Die literarische Zweiheit des Priester-Codex in der Genesis', *ZAW* 58 (1940–41), pp. 30-57 (46-48). McEvenue (*Narrative Style*, p. 147 n. 2) reiterates both von Rad's arguments, and, with evident approval, Humbert's criticism.
3.   Steuernagel (in 1920) had ascribed the passages to different P-strata; cf. C. Steuernagel, 'Bemerkungen zu Genesis 17', in *Festschrift Karl Budde* (BZAW, 34; Berlin: Töpelmann, 1920), pp. 172-79 (172, 177).
4.   Cf. Humbert, 'Die literarische Zweiheit', pp. 47-49.

part. The views in the ninth edition of his commentary on Genesis (1972) are fully reconcilable with those of Humbert. Although he is not very specific about the complexity of P, von Rad now seems to have abandoned his earlier thesis.[1] On the other hand, he does reaffirm that the chapter shows no uniformity in structure and content. Successive Priestly traditions about the covenant with Abraham are blended together, and the result is a theological composition, 'ein ganzes theologisches Korollarium'.[2] He also holds fast to the separation of vv. 15-22 from 1-14, but no longer sees them as parallel. Instead, the two passages taken together express a progressive salvation history ('der heilsgeschichtliche Fortschritt'). Verses 23-24 originally followed 1-15.[3]

E. Kutsch also recognizes secondary material in the chapter. In his view, vv. 3-5 should be taken together with 2 and 6; vv. 10-14 would then represent an originally separate regulation on how the circumcision should be performed. However, he denies the necessity of positing a different tradition for vv. 16-22. The whole section forms a united whole in which the promise to Abraham is extended to Isaac. Verse 22 concludes the section that begins in v. 1.[4]

S.R. Külling argues strongly in support of the original unity of Genesis 17. Unlike Humbert—with whom he otherwise agrees against von Rad—he sees in vv. 15-22 an amendment intended to define more clearly the content of the preceding part.[5] I myself do not see how his main argument for the unity of the chapter—the pact formula[6] would convincingly explain the mention of Ishmael in v. 20. His own effort to account for the mention of Ishmael shows his tendency towards harmonization.[7]

1. Cf. the remark by McEvenue, *Narrative Style*, p. 147 n. 4.
2. Cf. von Rad, *Genesis*, pp. 154, 159.
3. Cf. von Rad, *Genesis*, pp. 158-59.
4. Cf. E. Kutsch, '"Ich will euer Gott sein": b^erit in der Priesterschrift', *ZTK* 71 (1974), pp. 361-88 (373, 377, 382-83).
5. Cf. Külling, *Genesis-P-Stücke*, p. 260.
6. Cf. Külling, *Genesis-P-Stücke*, pp. 240-43.
7. Cf. Külling, *Genesis-P-Stücke*, p. 248. His efforts to vindicate the unity of the chapter—by asserting that circumcision does not mean actual inclusion in the specific promises of the covenant—falter in the light of vv. 9-14, which clearly does not warrant any such qualification. Other aspects of his conception of Gen. 17 do not invite serious consideration, for example, when he ranks the chapter in its present form among the oldest Old Testament texts!

Summary. The majority of scholars regard Genesis 17 as composite in character. Most source-critically oriented scholars would assign the middle section (vv. 15-22 with some variation) to a different, probably later, layer of tradition. Such a stratification overcomes the gap between vv. 14 and 23, which seem very much to belong together in accordance with the pattern of command and fulfilment seen in other P-texts (notably Gen. 1). Even if the fulfilment section here does not repeat the words of the command as exactly as Genesis 1, it is nonetheless clear from vv. 23 and 27 that the stipulations of the commandment are acted upon by Abraham:

The Command to Circumcise		Abraham Circumcised—	
v. 12	v. 13	23	26-27
'He that is eight days old'	—	'his son' —	—
'every male'		'every male'	'all the men of his house'
'[every male] born in your house'	'him that is born in your house'	'everyone born in his house'	'those born in the house'
'[every male who is] bought with money'	'[he that is] bought with your money'	'everyone bought with his money'	'and those bought with money. . . '

(The word-order of vv. 13, 23, 26 and 27 has been rearranged.)

The verses may follow a carefully worked-out system such as that proposed by N. Lohfink and supported by McEvenue.[1] The word 'foreigner' appears in the framing vv. 12 and 27 in the singular and without any suffixes. But if the beginning of the verses are included as well, the alleged system is not complete; v. 13 makes no reference to the 'eight days old' (the age of the son at circumcision), but jumps directly to the one born in the house. In this case v. 12 probably contained the original commandment, of which vv. 26-27 gave the account of the fulfilment (23 would seem to require 13 as its precedent).

---

1. Cf. N. Lohfink, 'Textkritisches zu Gn 17,5.13.16.17', *Bib* 48 (1967), pp. 439-42 (439). In order to obtain a fully chiastic system, Lohfink takes v. 13 from the Samaritan Version for v. 13: *ylydy* = v. 23. Cf. also McEvenue, *Narrative Style*, pp. 176-77.

Whatever the precise details, the general conclusions of source-criticism on the chapter would seem to justify focusing on vv. 15-21 and 23-27 for closer scrutiny (v. 22 belongs to the frame, as noted above).[1]

Verses 15-21. As shown by the division of the chapter above, Gen. 17.15-21 consists of two speeches by God. The passage also records Abraham's sceptical reaction to the message followed by an appeal on behalf of Ishmael. The section may be arranged in the following way:[2]

A	God speaks to Abraham and blesses Sarai; Abraham's reaction (vv. 15-18)
A.1	Introductory formula: 'And God said' (*wy'mr 'lhym*) to Abraham (15)
A.2	Message:
A.2.a	Sarai is to be called Sarah (16)
A.2.b	Blessing of Sarah: she will bear Abraham a son (16a), and many nations will arise from her (16b)
A.3	Abraham's reaction (17-18)
A.3.a	Emotional reactions: prostration, doubt (17)
A.3.b	Reaction uttered to God: petition concerning Ishmael (18)
B	God speaks to Abraham about Isaac and Ishmael (19-21)
B.1	Introductory formula: 'And God said' (*wy'mr 'lhym*) (19a)
B.2	Message (19b-c):
B.2.a	About Isaac:
	Sarah will bear you a son (19b)
	His name will be Isaac (19c)
	My covenant will be established with him (19d)

---

1.   As noted above, McEvenue opposes the majority opinion by asserting the unity of Gen. 17. His refusal to accept source-critical divisions seems unnecessary, since style can be imitated and artful composition does not exclude the use of earlier material on the part of the 'artist'. Literary artistry need hardly be the monopoly of any particular period of time, and nothing derogatory is implied about an artist's work simply because he or she happens to be at the end of a chain (as is the case with the work of the redactor behind Gen. 17). If, as McEvenue convincingly demonstrates, material from chs. 15 and 18 could be recast and worked into 17, then could not a later editor have made use of both P^g and P^s material?

2.   Cf. also Westermann, 'Genesis 17 und die Bedeutung von *berit*', pp. 163-65.

B.2.b	About Ishmael:
	Ishmael will be blessed (20a)
	He will multiply (20b)
	He will become a great nation (20c)
C	Repeated message concerning Isaac:
	Repetion of 19c (21a)
	Repetion of 19b, a (21b)

The intricate internal organization falls into two main parts, demonstrating a twofold interest on the part of the final redactor.[1] One is the assurance to Abraham that God's promise will be fulfilled, the other an interest in God's plans for Isaac and Ishmael.

Both A and B open with a similar reaffirmation to Abraham that he is to have a son. A.2 stresses God's initiative in the fulfilment—Sarah is merely God's instrument—'I will give you a son through her'. In B.2, on the other hand, Sarah's role is foregrounded. She is the rightful wife of Abraham; Isaac, by implication, is the legitimate heir: 'Sarah, your wife, shall bear you a son'. As the son of Abraham and Sarah, Isaac will be God's partner (*'ittô*) and instrument in the eternal covenant. God is the designer and sponsor of the covenant, speaking to Abraham and Sarah on behalf of all their future descendants—the people of Israel—whose whole destiny is involved in the coming birth.

It is from the perspective of Abraham's descendants that the fate and welfare of Ishmael (v. 20) is important. Ishmael will also be blessed and become a great nation. Verse 20 can be understood in the light of v. 18. 'I have heard you' is the answer to Abraham's plea, 'May Ishmael live before Thee!' (A.3.b). However, Abraham must understand that it is through Isaac, not Ishmael, that the promise will be fulfilled. Abraham's reaction, however natural—Ishmael is the son Abraham has before his eyes and is therefore of more immediate paternal concern—has to be curtailed. Throughout this passage Abraham appears as the sceptical realist rather than the obedient model believer who places all his trust in God (cf. Gen. 15.6 and Gen. 22, and also the picture of Abraham held by St Paul!).

Finally, in B.2.c, the message of v. 19 is repeated and summarized—covenant, name and birth—(in reverse order according to the chiasm).[2]

---

1. Cf. also McEvenue's treatment of the passage (*Narrative Style*, p. 174).
2. S. McEvenue (*Narrative Style*, p. 175) organizes the section differently. The chiasm AB—B'A' has an intermediate element C (v. 20) between A (19a; 21b) and B

In addition to these entangled internal relationships, the passage also refers to external material and echoes earlier traditions. With regard to Ishmael, P's sources are the Ishmael sections in chs. 16 and 21 (the latter generally ascribed to E, see below).[1] Verse 20 draws upon v. 16.10 and 21.(13)14-21. In 16.10 Hagar receives the promise that her seed will be very numerous. Here in 17.20, however, only the verb 'multiply' (*rbh*) is repeated, whereas its object, 'your seed'— already a theologically loaded term in the context of Genesis 16— refers directly to Ishmael. Gen. 17.20 adds the notion of 'blessing' ('I will bless him/Ishmael'). Thereby Ishmael is ranked with a very special group of people—the promise given to Abraham was also called a 'blessing' (12.2). A third announcement, 'I will make him fruitful', completes the message concerning Ishmael.

These announcements ('multiply him', 'bless him' and 'make him fruitful') may also be compared with God's order to the primeval humans in the P version of the creation story: 'Be fruitful [$p^e r\hat{u}$] and multiply [$r^e b\hat{u}$]' (Gen. 1.28).[2] This too is presented as a blessing: 'And God blessed them and said to them . . . ' The same verbs also appear together in the blessing of Jacob and Joseph by their respective fathers (Gen. 28.3; 48.4). Ishmael too will be blessed and become the progenitor of many descendants. In this respect he is the equal of Israel's own ancestors. As a result, P's refusal to include Ishmael in the covenant is all the more striking.

P's aim is to show Ishmael and his descendants branching off from Abraham and the people of Israel. It is through the two sons of Abraham that the division will take place that is necessary for the nation of Israel to emerge. This happens in a way which recalls how Cain was cut off from his family in Genesis 4. Cain and Ishmael are both driven away—one from Paradise, the other from the Promised Land—to beget new peoples in other lands. (Compare also the separation of Lot from Abraham.) But there is an essential difference between the fate of Cain and Ishmael. Ishmael is not guilty of any crime, and does not have to flee 'from the presence of Yahweh' as does Cain (Gen. 4.14). Indeed, ch. 21 promises that God will 'be with' Ishmael.

The comparison with Israel is underlined further by the prediction

(19b; 21a). To be complete, his arrangement would have to take in at least v. 18, to which v. 21 is a corollary.

1. This has been pointed out by McEvenue, *Narrative Style*, p. 154.
2. Cf. Westermann, *Genesis 12–36*, p. 325.

in v. 20 that 'a great nation' will arise from Ishmael[1] and that he will be 'a father of twelve princes'—just as Isaac will father a nation of twelve tribes through his son Jacob.[2] (Compare 25.12-16, where the names of the princes are listed.)[3] Ishmael will form a second and separate nation beside Israel; an 'Israel', as it were, without a Promised Land.

In all this, the idea of separation is prominent. It is obvious that the writer is concerned not just with the historical origin of the Ishmaelites,[4] but also with the theological distinction of Isaac–Israel from Ishmael. Ishmael is a separate nation and does not share in the prerogatives of God's elect people. (Indeed, in Priestly tradition, 'separation' seems to mean what 'election' means to the Deuteronomist and the prophets.) However, the motivation given to Abraham for saving Ishmael's life, 'because he is your offspring', indicates that, along with the idea of separation from Isaac, there was still a concern to preserve the link with Abraham. (In 21.18, as in 17.20, this idea is omitted, which suggests that these two passages stem from the same hand.)

Verses 23-27. This passage reports Abraham's faithful obedience to Yahweh's command. The report is wordy and repetitious, and the compound nature of the passage is evident. It consists of at least two separate reports added together (v. 23; vv. 26-27), which should be treated in isolation from the context of vv. 15-21(22). Verses 23-27 conflict with v. 20. Verses 23 and 26 have Ishmael circumcised by Abraham together with all his household. Because in vv. 10-11 the circumcision was explicitly prescribed as the mark of the covenant, Ishmael is now, to all intents and purposes, included in the covenant.[5]

1. Ishmael is also called a 'nation' in 21.13 (several scholars would read 'great nation', as in 17.20); cf. Westermann, *Genesis 12–36*, p. 417.

2. The use of the number twelve together with the word 'prince' suggests to Westermann and others an allusion to the *Stammesspruch*. Cf. Westermann, *Genesis 12–36*, p. 325, and his references to de Vaux and Speiser.

3. Cf. B. Dicou, *Jakob en Esau, Israël en Edom: Israël tegenover de volken in de verhalen over Jakob en Esau in Genesis en in de grote profetieën over Edom* (Voorburg: Publivorm, 1990), p. 55.

4. Although this, together with its theological implications, seems to be the main point for Westermann, *Genesis 12–36*, p. 325.

5. Cf. Westermann's remark, 'Genesis 17', p. 170, against E. Kutsch, '"Ich will euer Gott sein"', p. 383. But Kutsch is right insofar as his observation refers to

And in turn, Abraham's obedience to the command in vv. 12-13 is in conflict with God's own words in vv. 19 and 21. The inclusion of Ishmael in vv. 23 and 26 cannot in any way be reconciled with the previous verses. This problem does not seem to have been fully realized by McEvenue, which seriously undermines his understanding of the chapter.

Blum wants to preserve the continuity between vv. 19-22 and 23-27 by an appeal to 'die innere Logik des Textes'; Ishmael had to be circumcised, since he belonged to the house of Abraham. According to Blum, his circumcision is intended as a sign of the covenant for Abraham himself. I can only accept Blum's view regarding the 'inner logic of the text' for vv. 9-14, 23-27. However, it is difficult to resort to this logic for vv. 19-21, since it is exactly and explicitly Ishmael's standing in relation to the covenant—his *exclusion* from it—that is at issue here. The tacit question behind v. 20 is: 'what, then, will become of Ishmael?', and the contradiction is certainly not simply 'presumed'.[1]

In addition to the 'literary' function of Gen. 17.23-27 as the corollary to the commandment in vv. 10-11, it also shows an 'inclusive' attitude towards Ishmael as a member of Abraham's family. He is the first to be circumcised in Abraham's household, which, at that point, consists only of his servants and Ishmael. The Ishmael of v. 23 is a *primus inter pares*. His equals are the marginal groups of household slaves. The Ishmael of Gen. 17.23-27 is still the only *son* of Abraham, but that status is soon to be changed with the birth of Isaac.

In a way he is already a stand-in for Isaac. He is circumcised as Abraham's 'son', if only because the circumcision is instituted before the birth of Isaac. Verse 23 is regulatory; it gives the precedent for all future generations to follow: the father has to circumcise his son and his servants. But with Ishmael, Abraham is of course unable to meet the demand that the son be circumcised on his eighth day. That will only be possible with Isaac (21.4). Ishmael therefore holds an ambiguous rank between that of his father and of a slave.

For the marginal groups in Israel, circumcision was the criterion of participation in such things as the Passover celebrations (Exod. 12.43-49). In this respect, at least, the circumcision raised them to the rank

vv. 19-21. I cannot find in 19-21 any substantiation for Westermann's contention that the promise to Ishmael is called *bᵉrît*. Cf. also Humbert, 'Die literarische Zweiheit', p. 50.

1. Cf. Blum, *Vätergeschichte*, p. 422, including n. 15.

of 'a native of the land' (Exod. 12.48). Ishmael is not 'born in the house', but he is still a son, albeit of a slave, and under such circumstances he holds an intermediate position between the family proper and the servants. His position between Israelite and slave-foreigner might have become important when Israel had to live among foreigners. Ishmael was associated with Egypt through his mother and by marriage (Gen. 21.21; cf. also 37.25). Deut. 23.8(7) mentions Edom (Esau) and Egypt together as the two foreign peoples allowed into the assembly of the Lord:

> You shall not abhor an Edomite, for he is your brother; you shall not abhor an Egyptian, because you were a sojourner in his land (Deut. 23.7, RSV).

The favoured status of Edom and Egypt (in contrast to the Ammonites and the Moabites) is, as von Rad remarks, difficult to explain on historical grounds.[1] The reasons given in the text are specific and refer back to the origins of Israel. Edom is a 'brother', and in Egypt, Israel itself lived as *ger*. The *ger* inside Israel's boundaries was a reminder of the time spent as *ger* in Egypt. As Edom was Israel's 'brother', so Ishmael was Israel's 'half-brother'—representing Egypt in the communal memory. The very formal language of Gen. 17.23-27 may express a similar attitude in the Priestly tradition. The origin of the formal inclusion of Ishmael in the passage may have been the postexilic renaissance of Israel's history represented by Chronicles. In Van Seters's interpretation, the chapter represents a move towards reconstructing the religion of Israel for the needs of the postexilic society, allowing, for example, for proselytism among the peoples of diaspora.[2] I shall return to this point when considering the theological implications of Genesis 17 below.

Summary
Gen. 17.23-27 can be taken as a retrojection of later conditions in Israel back into the lifetime of Abraham. These conditions involved questions about circumcision as an absolute prerequisite for being counted among the true children of Abraham. Through circumcision

---

1. G. von Rad (*Das fünfte Buch Mose Deuteronomium übersetzt und erklärt* [ATD, 8; Göttingen: Vandenhoeck & Ruprecht, 1964], p. 104) tends towards an explanation in terms of cult, but I fail to see how Lev. 21.16-18 would illuminate the matter.
2. Cf. J. Van Seters, *Abraham*, p. 293.

the marginal groups were allowed into the religious community of Israel. (St Paul's arguments in Gal. 5.6 and 6.12 certainly run counter to the intentions of the Priestly writer behind ch. 17.)

Gen. 17.19-21, on the other hand, must be judged against the background of times when Israel's religious (and national) identity was endangered by foreigners from within (as exemplified in Neh. 13) as well as from without.[1] Verses 19-21 would then be an understandable reaction by a redactor concerned about the purity of Israel. It is possible that such a redactor, writing in a postexilic time, would dream of a new beginning, a new creation and a new scattering of peoples throughout the world, as in the first beginning. Isaac and Ishmael would then represent the new nations originating from Abraham, the 'second Adam'. Such an outlook is not far from that of Deutero-Isaiah, a point on which I shall elaborate in my theological evaluation of the Ishmael sections.

The upshot of this must be that the two Ishmael sections in Genesis 17 attest two different attitudes towards him: one exclusive, the other inclusive. This inherent paradox is thrown into sharp relief against a postexilic background. After the upheavals of the exile, the Israelite community had to come to terms with radically changed conditions affecting its life and institutions. At the same time, however, its old beliefs and time-honoured practices had to be safeguarded. The new prospects opening up in the outside world had to be understood by looking back within its own traditions and religious inheritance.

---

1. It is notable that, in a text supposed to relate the early days of Israel in its own land, the name of Ishmael is left out. In Joshua's recollection of Israel's past (Josh. 24.3), only Isaac is mentioned as Abraham's son, given by God, although both Jacob and Esau are mentioned together in v. 4. This may reflect a period when it was necessary to guard against foreign influence and to consolidate Israel's own achievements (note also, incidentally, that here it is through Jacob and his family, in line with the Joseph story, that the connection to Egypt is made).

Genesis 21

Structure and Content
Chapter 21 contains four sections:

     I.a   The Birth of Isaac (1-7)
     I.b   Abraham's banquet on the occasion of the weaning of Isaac (8)
     II   9-21 (see below)
     III   Abraham and Abimelech (22-32)
     IV   Abraham at Beersheba (33-34)

As this division demonstrates, the contents of ch. 21 are extremely diverse. The first two sections deal with Abraham's family affairs, while the third reports a dispute between Abraham and Abimelech over a well and the subsequent pact between them. This third section seems rather loosely attached to those previous. The only element in common with vv. 1-21 is the existence of a well, the word for 'well of water' being the same in vv. 19 and 25. As in 16.14, the etymology of the well's name is appended to the preceeding story; although here the name is not theophoric but linked to the taking of an oath (v. 31; it may be that the *'el 'ôlām* of v. 33 relates to this well in the same way as *'el rō'î* does to the well of 16.13-14. If that is the case, the invocation of Yahweh by Abraham would parallel Hagar's prayer in 16.13).

The overall character of the chapter is narrative, and this alone justifies a comparison with ch. 16 rather than 17. As I have already shown, vv. 3-5 is of a similar origin to 16.15-16,[1] and the whole of section Ia must be understood in accordance with the pattern of promise–fulfilment (the birth of a son to Abraham and Sarah) and commandment–compliance (the covenant and the circumcision) that runs through the preceding chapters. As pointed out by Westermann, the section refers back to Gen. 11.27-32, and thus it concludes a principal episode in the Abraham cycle. Isaac is the central figure. He is the son in whom God's promise reaches its fulfilment and through whom God's command that the eldest son be circumcised on the eighth day is fully complied with for the first time in Israel's history (v. 4; cf. 17.12). Ishmael is not mentioned at all in these verses, and when he does appear he is seen by Sarah and by God (10, 12) as a potential challenger of Isaac's rights.[2] Again, as in 17.18-19, Isaac and Ishmael

---

1.   Cf. Westermann, *Genesis 12–36*, p. 405.
2.   Bar-Efrat (*Narrative Art*, p. 73) remarks that God's words in vv. 12-13 are

are competitors, but and now in a more direct way than in 16.5, where the rivalry is mediated through the two mothers-to-be.

Verses 9-21

It is not until v. 9 that Ishmael enters the scene, and so it is section II which is of immediate concern here. Verse 8 links section I and II, simultaneously ending section I and beginning section II.[1] Verse 9 implies that it is during the party in v. 8 that Sarah suddenly realizes the threat posed to Isaac by the very presence of Hagar's son. Verse 8a, 'the child grew up', corresponds to vv. 20-21 in section II—'God was with the lad and he grew up . . . '; both are conventional summary formulas (which also represent a kind of embryonic childhood story) leading up to the next important episode in the narrative. Section II may be subdivided as follows:

A   Sarah initiates and brings about the expulsion of Hagar and Ishmael (9-11)

A.1   Sarah observes and acts (*wtr' śrh—wt'mr*, 9-10)

A.2   Abraham's reaction and God's answer:
        A.2.a.   Abraham's reaction (11)
        A.2.b.   God's speech (12-13)

A.3   Abraham expels Hagar and Ishmael

B   Hagar and Ishmael in the desert (15-19)

B.1   Hagar and Ishmael abandoned and in need of help (15-16)

B.2   God's reaction and the Angel's speech
        B.2.a   God intervenes (17ab)
        B.2.b   The Angel's speech (17c-18)

B.3   Deliverance by provision of water (19)

C   Ishmael's biography (20-21)

Part C is obviously intended as the final word on Ishmael's later fortunes, but since v. 20 would be quite sufficient for this purpose, v. 21 is probably an addition from some later stage,[2] intended to establish for him an Egyptian connection apart from his mother. It specifies the 'wilderness' where he lives (v. 20) as 'the wilderness of Paran' on the

---

devoid of the disdain evident in Sarah's. Of more importance, however, is the fact that God completely endorses Sarah's intiative to cast out Hagar and her son: 'Do as she tells you' (12).

1. Cf. Kilian, *Abrahamsüberlieferungen*, p. 231; Van Seters, *Abraham*, p. 196.

2. So also Kilian, *Abrahamsüberlieferungen*, p. 235; v. 21 is an *interpretament* of 20b. Cf. also Westermann, *Genesis 12–36*, p. 420.

way to Egypt (which broadly corresponds to the information in 25.18), and provides him with an Egyptian wife, which will in turn allow him to father 'a great nation'. Verse 21 would then achieve the same end as vv. 25.12-17, which lists Ishmael's descendants and is traditionally assigned to P. Verse 21 may also have been added as an analogy with the fate of Cain. Gen. 4.16 refers both to Cain's area of habitation ('lived in the land of Nod', and 'he lived in the wilderness of Paran') and, in the following verse, to his wife. Similarly, both passages mention Cain's and Ishmael's occupations, although in Cain's case a special point lies in the fact that he, 'the tiller of ground' (Gen. 4.2), is driven away from the ground and has to leave his occupation. Ishmael, too, is driven away, but for other reasons.

From my arrangement of the section, it seems that A and B have a similar structure: the 'situation' (which sets the problem) in 1 is followed by the reaction and speech in 2, after which the 'solution' is found. In A.1 it is Sarah who first perceives the danger; in B.1 it is Hagar. In A.2 Abraham's reaction causes Yahweh to speak, but in B.2 he intervenes directly on Hagar's behalf. Common to A and B is the speech in 2.b, which prepares for the solution in 3. The common structure underlines how differently the persons involved fared. Verse 20 thus emphazises the paradox: God is not only with Isaac, but also with the wretched Ishmael! Of course this structure would only have emerged at the final stage of the composition, and so the pre-history of the passage must also be considered.

Part B differs from A in respect of its genre, since B exhibits all the important ingredients of a miracle-story, such as the plight which befalls the protagonists, the measures taken, help received from God, description of the rescue and its result, and so on. Part A does not contain any corresponding elements.

Verse 15, 'When the water in the skin was gone . . .', sets the course for Hagar's ensuing action. In this case her action does not conform to that in similar situations in the same genre. In other miracle stories the suffering person seeks help from a man of God. Here she expresses her despair as she is about to die. Without any request from Hagar, God intervenes: 'God heard the voice [of the lad]' (v. 17). The saving act is indicated by the words 'God opened up her eyes'; in other words, she discovers what has been there all the time.

Kilian holds 21.9-21 to be the result of a successive accumulation of

material which, accordingly, he arranges in three layers (not sources).[1]
The basic layer comprised vv. 17a, c, 18b, 19a, b and 20. This was
later expanded in two separate phases, and it was only in the second
phase that the Elohist was at work. The basic layer, the *Grundschrift*,
represented an Ishmael tradition, an earlier form of which had
already been used in 16.11-14—hence, Kilian argues, the similarities
between the two chapters. The first phase created a full story, the
story of Hagar's rejection, out of disparate earlier material. This phase
also saw the joining together of the Abraham and the old Ishmael
traditions. As a result, Kilian's presumes, as I do, that 21.9-21 is not a
coherent unit. I also share Kilian's overall understanding of the compositional process of the chapter as a cumulative process, although I
disagree with him over the details, as will become clear.

Westermann suggests that God's speech to Hagar (17-18) is composite. It is based on two different revelation formulas: the salvation
oracle (*Heilsorakel*) and the announcement of a messenger of God
(*Botschaft eines Gottesboten*). He regroups the material in the
following way:[2]

1. The Messenger's Announcement	2. The Salvation Oracle
The Angel of the Lord	
'What troubles you, Hagar?'	'Fear not, for God has heard
'Arise, lift up the lad'	the voice of the lad'
	'I will make him a great nation'

From a comparison with other texts, it seems that the question 'what
troubles you/what is the matter with you?' (*mâ lāk*) belongs in the
context of dialogues where information is asked for, for example, in a
particular predicament or when some further specification of a wish is
demanded. Such is the case with the woman of Samaria in 2 Kgs 6.26-
29, who asks the king of Israel for help:

> A woman cried out to him, saying: 'Help, my lord, O king!'. . . And the
> king asked her: 'What is your trouble?' She answered . . .

She then gives information on the events leading up to the present
situation. Likewise, in 1 Sam. 11.5 Saul asks the elders of Jabesh, 'What
ails the people (*mâ lā'ām*), that they are weeping?', and he is told of
the impending danger. In Isa. 22.1 the question is a rhetorical one and

---

1. Cf. Kilian, *Abrahamsüberlieferungen*, pp. 236-38, 247; also the synopsis,
248-50.
2. Cf. Westermann, *Genesis 12–36*, pp. 257-60, 419.

accordingly receives no immediate answer: 'What do you mean (*mâ lāk*) that you have gone up, all of you, to the roofs . . . ' Finally, in Judg. 1.14, Caleb asks his daughter, 'What do you wish [*mâ lāk*)?', and the girl states her wish in answer.

In Gen. 21.17 the question receives no immediate answer (although it is not rhetorical). The answer to the question has already been expressed by the 'voice of the lad' which provoked God to react: 'God has heard the voice of the lad where he is'.

God's answer begins with the words, 'Fear not!', which, as Westermann points out, is a common phrase in Deutero-Isaiah, but it also appears earlier on in Genesis (15.1). The same expression occurs with the same function in 2 Kgs 6.17, in which the words are spoken by Elisha to his servant on discovering the horses and chariots sent by the king of Syria:

> 'Fear not, for those who are with us are more than those who are with them'. Then Elisha prayed, and said, 'O Lord, I pray thee, open his eyes that he may see'. So the Lord opened the eyes of the young man, and he saw; and behold, the mountain was full of horses and chariots of fire round about Elisha.

Here too, as with Hagar, an opening of the eyes is seen as an act of God.

God's opening of Hagar's eyes is a marvelous saving act. She receives help directly from God that proves that 'God was with [Ishmael]' (v. 20). In other words, it is not a question of a miracle involving natural or physical upheavals[1] nor of the glorification of a 'man of God', but rather a reassurance of God's active presence with Hagar and her son.

I propose, then, that this miracle story originally formed an independent unit which was later combined with the previous section. The presence of the angel would suggest that E was responsible ('the Angel of God from heaven' is generally taken as a mark of the Elohist; cf. 22.11). In the terms of traditional source criticism, the Angel's speech to Hagar was a later addition by E, which would either have appeared in a very different form, or else would have been missing altogether in the original story. The effect of the addition was to emphasize the emotional and the miraculous elements often present in E texts

---

1.   Cf. von Rad, *Genesis*, p. 185.

(notably Exod. 3–5; 7–10).[1] In this way, a new and unified account was created out of two disparate stories. The new story served a double purpose: first, it explained how Hagar came to be in the desert; secondly, it accounted for the final separation between Isaac and Ishmael. (The two brothers never meet again, and there is no reunion such as that between Jacob and Esau in the J–E tradition, although, according to P, they meet at the burial of Abraham, 25.6.) The compositional stages of B can then be delineated as follows:

> 1. The story of Hagar and Ishmael's expulsion (v. 14); God commands and Abraham obeys. Result: 'she departed and lived in the wilderness of Beer-sheba'.
>
> 2. A story about Hagar and Ishmael in the desert.

(In both stories, Ishmael is still a child whom Hagar can carry on her shoulders [14] and 'cast' under a bush [15].)

> 3. Expansion (E):
>   a. The combination of 1-2 into one unit.
>   b. God's intervention and speech to Hagar (vv. 17-18). Result: 'God was with the lad' (20a).
>
> 4. Supplement (P):
>   a. Ishmael grows up, lives in the wilderness, becomes an archer (20bc).
>   b. Ishmael's life and marriage (21).
>
> 5. A gloss: 'I will make him a great nation' (18c).

(The gloss repeats and reinforces the point of v. 13.)[2]

The second element (2) draws on similar tradition to the story in 16.7-14. Most commentators regard chs. 16 and 21 as different versions of the same story.[3] Westermann's hypothesis of an *Ergänzer* behind vv. 8-21 (see above) makes him more sceptical.[4] Blum thinks that Gen. 21.8-21 represents a version of a parallel tradition to ch. 16 that 'competed' with it. This transformation permited a syntagmatic arrangement of the two texts into one narrative sequence. Van Seters

1. Cf. Skinner, *Genesis*, p. xlviii.
2. Cf. Westermann, *Genesis 12–36*, p. 419.
3. Cf. Gunkel, *Genesis*, pp. 231-33; von Rad, *Genesis*, p. 186; Skinner, *Genesis*, p. 324; Kilian, *Abrahamsüberlieferungen*, p. 243.
4. Cf. Westermann, *Genesis 12–36*, pp. 413-14; he also notes some discrepancies between the two chapters; cf. p. 415.

stands out by considering ch. 21 to be dependent on ch. 16.[1]

However one may arrange Genesis 16 and 21, it is important to note that when the story in 16 begins (v. 7) Hagar is already in the desert. This was probably the case with the version in ch. 21 as well, in which case 21.14 and 15 would originally have been separate, in accordance with my own theory of the compositional process given above. Gen. 16.6 does not specify where Hagar fled; only in v. 7 are we informed that she was in the desert. Gen. 21.14, on the other hand, gives the name of the desert, 'the wilderness of Beer-sheba'. In source-critical terms, J and E would have known quite different versions of the same episode: in 16 (J) Hagar flees alone; in 21 (E) she is driven away from the household of Abraham together with her child. However, in both versions it is clear that her expulsion follows as a consequence of a quarrel with Sarah,[2] and that this forms the logical conclusion to the preceding episode rather than the beginning of the next one (the events in the desert).

Story 1 would have related the quarrel, Sarah's aggravation and Hagar's expulsion. Story 2, in common with 16.7-14, would have reflected a common experience in ancient times: a desert-wanderer dying of thirst suddenly discovering a well or oasis. Such experiences would have been open to a religious interpretation, as a revelation from the demon of the well or the like (see on ch. 16 above and the similar situation in 1 Kgs 19.3-8).[3] Jacob's case shows that wayfaring was a timely occasion for encounters with divine beings, and such a background is highly likely for the story of Hagar in the desert. (On the well in ch. 16, see above.)

Ishmael in Verses 9-21
This miracle-story is a clear reflection of Israel's kinship with peoples of the desert, but it is unlikely that 'Ishmael' would represent any specific, identifiable tribe. The fact that the name of Ishmael might, on purely etymological grounds, be connected with some known tribal

---

1.   Van Seters, *Abraham*, pp. 197, 200, 202; Blum, *Vätergeschichte*, pp. 312-15. Part of Blum's argument is based on the parallels he finds between chs. 21 and 22 under the theme 'Abraham looses his son' (cf. p. 314).

2.   Cf. Zucker, 'Conflicting Conclusions', p. 44.

3.   O.H. Steck (*Überlieferung und Zeitgeschichte in den Elia-Erzählungen* [WMANT, 20; Neukirchen–Vluyn: Neukirchener Verlag, 1968], p. 27 n. 5) thinks that a local (*ortsgebunden*) tradition was applied in both Gen. 21 and 1 Kgs 19.

group cannot be decisive for the understanding of this story (see above). Rather, it should be understood as another demonstration of Yahweh's mercy towards the weak and discarded.

Of special interest is the picture given of Ishmael as an individual. In A he is the 'son of the slave-woman' (v. 10), both in the mouth of Sarah (as against 'my son Isaac', 10) and of God (13). At the same time, he is Abraham's 'son' and 'seed' (11, 13). As son of the slave woman, he is the object of Sarah's hatred and is denied the same status as her own son. In contrast, as son of Abraham, he is entitled to partake of the promises given to the Patriarch. Abraham, troubled by the lot of his son, is consoled in v. 13, as in 17.20, with the promise of a future for Ishmael as 'a great nation'. Although the bonds between Abraham and his genealogical line through Hagar will be severed, he will still gain descendants by it. The issue here is not whether Ishmael will be included in or excluded from the covenant, as it is in 17.20-21, but who will carry on the name of Abraham. When 21.12-13 are taken together, the outcome of the 'competition' between Isaac and Ishmael is essentially the same as in 17.21; Ishmael cannot share the same status as Isaac. He has to be removed before he is able to make any serious claims to his rights as heir and son of Abraham. Only in separation from Isaac will he be able to take advantage of his position as heir of Abraham and become a nation.

By contrast, in section B God's care for Ishmael manifests itself not in the words of a 'promise' in general, but in a specific saving act. God ensures that Ishmael has a future. (To make this explicit, the gloss in v. 18 was added.) The fact that God 'was with' Ishmael indicates that God is still the guarantor of the promise even to the expelled Ishmael.

Theologically, B is significant as another demonstration of God's concern for the outcast which appears repeatedly throughout the pages of the Bible. God cares about widows and orphans, the slave and the foreigner, the 'outsider' in general. In this sense the story in B evokes memories of Israel's own past. During their desert wanderings, the Israelites themselves experienced similar marvelous acts, and whenever the people of Israel dared to forget, they were rebuked:

... you forget Yahweh, your God ... who led you through the great and terrible wilderness, with its fiery serpents and scorpions and thirsty ground where there was no water, who brought you water out of the flinty rock.[1]

This is also recalled by Hosea (13.5):

It was I who knew you in the desert, in the land of burning heat ...

But in the end, an essential difference existed between Israel and Ishmael: Israel's time in the desert was only a station on the way from Egypt to the Promised Land; Ishmael was to remain in the desert, to make it his home.

Summary

The Hagar story in ch. 21 is a mixture of different elements combined by a redactor, generally understood to be E. Subsequently it was turned into a miracle story, with the expulsion being reduced to a prelude. It is only through God's intervention that Hagar and Ishmael survive as a sign that God himself is willing to answer for Ishmael, to 'be with' him.

In view of the composition of vv. 9-21, the effect of the expulsion of Hagar and her son in story 1 (A) is allayed by story 2 (B); it is not, after all, God's last word on the matter. The theological significance of the story in B can be summarized as follows:

1. The figure of Ishmael depicts an 'incomplete' Israel, an Israel, that is, which never attains the land of the promise.
2. Ishmael, belonging nowhere and a stranger even in the land of his birth, could be looked upon as patron of the various marginal groups on the outskirts of Israelite society: the foreigners, the slaves and the sojourners.
3. The Ishmael section should also be viewed in relation to Genesis 22.[2] Isaac too is brought to the point of death, only to be saved by God's intervention. Being a son of Abraham preserves neither Ishmael nor Isaac from trials and danger.

---

1. Deut. 8.14-16, referring to Massah and Meribah, Exod. 17; compare also Exod. 15.22-27.
2. Cf. above on 21.9-21, and Sternberg, *Poetics*, p. 132.

Both of them, regardless of their final status, undergo a very similar start in life, and God intervenes to save both of them from destruction.

Genesis 25

Structure and Content

Chapter 25 places Ishmael in a much wider context than the previous texts. Now he is a child of Abraham, not one of two, but one of many sons, and like these he is the ancestor of several other tribes. Here, all of Abraham's children appear as equals.

First there is a section on Keturah, Abraham's second wife (vv. 1-6).[1] She is introduced here for the first time, and the whole passage is probably secondary.[2]

Verses 1-6

In v. 6, the sons of Abraham's concubines are dealt with; they receive gifts and are then sent away from Isaac. Again, the idea of separation between Isaac and the other sons of Abraham is underlined—and all the more in that this happens during Abraham's lifetime. Isaac receives everything that belongs to Abraham (*'t-kl-'šr-lw*, v. 5); Ishmael and the others receive only complimentary gifts, nothing they can claim in their own right. That the sons of Keturah are 'sent away' need not be seen as a deliberate imitation of ch. 21,[3] but rather as an explanation of why they are never mentioned again in the story of Isaac. Verse 6 was also probably intended to explain the presence of other tribes, speaking similar languages, on the borders of Israel and beyond.

These verses are marked by a much broader geographical perspective as well as a more universalistic attitude. The discrimination between Isaac and the other 'sons' seems sharper here than in the previous passages, and the whole section is probably very late—a retrojection

---

1. Westermann (*Genesis 12–36*, p. 484) denies that the word *'šh* for 'wife' is important here. Note, however, that Hagar is also called *'šh* when she is first given to Abraham in 16.3; whereas elsewhere she is merely called 'maid' (*'mh* or *šphh*). Both Hagar and Keturah are referred to as 'concubines' (*pylgšym*) in 25.6.

2. Cf. Westermann, *Genesis 12–36*, pp. 483-84. The source-critical character of the passage is unclear; cf. Kilian, *Abrahamsüberlieferungen*, pp. 282-83.

3. So Westermann, *Genesis 12–36*, p. 485.

of postexilic conditions when Israel had become keenly aware of the
organization of the world around.

Verses 7-11

This second section relates the age, death and burial of Abraham in
the usual style of P (cf. 35.28-29). Isaac is now joined by Ishmael at
the burial of their father, exactly as Esau and Jacob will come
together to bury their father Isaac. Here again, Ishmael is an equal of
Isaac. The author has completely lost sight of (or ignores) ch. 21,[1] in
which Ishmael's expulsion is intended to be absolute. The mention of
Ishmael here is probably based on convention (in view of 35.29 he
should have been mentioned before Isaac). Abraham must receive a
decent burial by both his sons.

Verse 11 contradicts 17.20: only Isaac is blessed by God. In addition,
the mention of Isaac's living place seems awkward. Gen. 16.14 implies
that Beer-lahai-roi is the name of Ishmael's birthplace. The remark
here seems loosely attached, and I would be willing, along with a
number of scholars,[2] to transpose it to follow 24.67. (In 24.62 Isaac
comes from Beer-lahai-roi to meet Rebecca in the Negeb.)

Verses 12-18

Verse 12 introduces a new section, generally ascribed to P, which gives
the names of Ishmael's sons.[3] The number twelve for the princes of
Ishmael is taken by von Rad to imply an ampichtyonic organization
for the Ishmaelites, like that alleged for the tribes of Israel. This is
unfounded, not only because it relies on the outdated ampichtyony
hypothesis, but also in taking the list to reflect first-hand historical
knowledge. It is difficult to see how the list could be related to other
material of known historical value, apart from studies in comparative
eponymology; but not all the names are attested outside the Old
Testament.[4] As Westermann also points out,[5] it is merely a list of
names primarily of geographical significance.

---

1.   So Westermann, *Genesis 12–36*, p. 486; cf. also von Rad, *Genesis*, p. 210.
2.   So Gunkel, *Genesis*, p. 260; Westermann, *Genesis 12–36*, p. 486; Van
Seters, *Abraham*, p. 248.
3.   It is possible that the list of names comes from pre-P tradition; so
Westermann, *Genesis 12–36*, pp. 483, 486.
4.   Cf. Westermann, *Genesis 12–36*, p. 487.
5.   Cf. Westermann, *Genesis 12–36*, p. 483.

However, there may be a theological point to von Rad's comparison with Israel. The list is a demonstration, similar to 17.20, that God's promise to Ishmael was fulfilled; he became the progenitor of many nations. 'Twelve' would then be the fulfilment of the promise of 'many', imitating the tribal organization of Israel.[1]

Summary
Gen. 25.1-18 represents the beginnings of a 'narrowing of focus' on the children of Israel. Here, 'the children of Abraham' are a wider entity and include peoples with whom the family of Isaac and Jacob had little or no contact. The composition of the chapter must be quite late, since it reflects the arrangement of the first part of the book of Genesis in its shift in vv. 19-20 from a universal perspective down to the life story of Isaac. Abraham is a 'second Adam' ushering in a new generation of peoples in the lands of the Bible.

---

1.   The term *haṣrêhem* in v. 16 corresponds to the Mari term *ḥasarum* denoting a nomadic settlement; cf. Van Seters, *Abraham*, p. 18; Westermann, *Genesis 12-36*, p. 488.

Chapter 2

THE ISHMAEL MOTIF APPLIED TO A POSTEXILIC CONTEXT

The Roots: Ishmael in the Sources

Ishmael features in four chapters of Genesis: 16, 17, 21 and 25. He appears in contexts ranging from narration to genealogy and theological treatise. Traditional source criticism disburses this material among the three main Tetrateuchal sources: ch. 16 is ascribed to J, 21 to E, and 17, 25 and parts of 16 to P. This would suggest the existence of an extensive Ishmael tradition which may be explained in the following way. Some Ishmael material may well have been included in the early stages of biblical tradition,[1] and the figure of Ishmael then lingered on in the sources down to postexilic times. Such a tradition probably originated with the nomadic groups in and around Canaan, who were affected by the Israelite settlement. It was subsequently gathered together and integrated with the Abraham–Isaac cycle. In the process Ishmael was made Isaac's half-brother and competitor for the legacy of Abraham.

An explanation along such lines would fit the customary appraisal of the patriarchal narratives either as 'family stories' (Westermann),[2] or as representing the experiences of a whole tribe. In the first case, the Ishmael–Isaac material would be an apt illustration of conflicts within the family: wife versus concubine, brother versus (half)brother, and

1. For example, Kilian (*Abrahamsüberlieferungen*, pp. 84-87) hints at the possibility of an Ishmaelitic tradition.
2. Westermann's application of A. Jolles's ideas to the biblical material receives critical attention in J.W. Rogerson, *Anthropology and the Old Testament* (Oxford: Basil Blackwell, 1978), pp. 73-76. Cf. also J.P. Fokkelman, *Narrative Art in Genesis: Specimens of Stylistic and Structural Analysis* (Studia Semitica Neerlandica, 17; Assen: Van Gorcum, 1975), p. 86. In Fokkelman's words, Jolles's use of the term 'saga' has become 'common property' in Old Testament scholarship. He notes, however, the criticism raised by Richter and Koch.

so on. In the second case, the Ishmael stories would explain the early history of the 'Ishmaelites'.

Having analyzed the various Ishmael passages, I find it difficult to accept suggestions of an originally independent Ishmael tradition behind the biblical sources. The evidence of an independent tradition is tenuous, and quite insufficient to support the existence of an identifiable Ishmaelite tribe. As I have said above, it is remarkable how passive Ishmael is in the texts. He is constantly referred to in relation to others, mainly Isaac. He is seldom connected with an effectively transitive verb, and he never appears as a speaking or reflecting subject. This applies especially to chs. 17 and 16 (11-12), in which his birth is announced. These include two literary *Gattungen* common in the Old Testament—the annunciation and the tribal oracle. This would make it unlikely that they referred to any existing individuals.[1] By its very nature, the *Stammesspruch* employs language peculiar to the genre, although it allows for a certain degree of individualization, such as in the animal metaphor, for example. Even so, Ishmael does not stand out as a person with his own distinctive qualities. Again, in ch. 21, as in 17, his fortunes are in every respect conditioned by the presence of Isaac. Ishmael is not entitled to a position alongside Isaac (v. 10), even if, as son of Abraham, he is granted certain favours (17.20; 21.13). The lurking conflict with Isaac is a more forceful argument for expelling him from his own family than are the bonds with Abraham for letting him stay. The story about Hagar and Ishmael shows him weak and forlorn, dependent upon his mother and ultimately upon the intervention of God. Likewise ch. 25 provides no support for the existence of separate Ishmael traditions. Verses 12-16 are a projection back into history of names and conditions from much later times. They reflect an effort to organize the surrounding world in relation to Israel, and to create an image of a new world, following a new covenant in ch. 17, of more limited scope than the post-deluge world of Genesis 10, itself preceded by the new covenant with Noah in ch. 9. Abraham is the forefather of three Semitic clans through Keturah, Hagar and Sarah, as was Noah of the three primaeval clans.

Whatever the origin of the figure of Ishmael, and however powerless as a character, his role was nevertheless regarded as important enough to justify his inclusion in the Abraham and Isaac cycles. One

---

1. The etymology in v. 11c is very probably a secondary insertion.

reason for that inclusion may be found in comparison with Cain and Esau (and possibly Lot).[1] There is always someone who parts company with, or is pushed aside from, the community of the nearest kinsmen. Ishmael has to play this role in relation to Isaac, as does Esau to Jacob. But in the case of Ishmael in ch. 21, his departure is sanctioned by God (v. 12)—although it is not explicitly incited; while Ishmael remains passive, Cain and Esau are directly involved in the chain of events that culminates in their departure.

Above all, it is in 17.19-21 and 21.12-13 that the issue of Ishmael's destiny becomes acute. These five verses are divine answers given at a time when Abraham has to make a choice that is to prove crucial for Israel's future. Everything in the context suggests that Abraham will make the wrong decision and let matters remain as they are (17.18). In fact, the choice has already been made by God, and Abraham only has to be convinced. These verses disclose what could best be termed an 'Ishmael theology'. This theology, a hallmark of the Priestly writings, reflects a crisis in the life of Abraham. He has to face the consequences of the earlier and seemingly well-advised decision to make Hagar the bearer of his offspring. Later, once Sarah has also borne him a son, Yahweh's original promise that Abraham would become father of many nations (17.4, 5; cf. 12.2) must now be doubly fulfilled. Yet, although he will be the father of many nations, there will be only one covenant, the covenant between Isaac and Yahweh (17.19, 21). Once that covenant has been established, Ishmael's position becomes problematic and has to be reappraised.

The Development: A Theological Appraisal of Ishmael

Genesis 15 sets the background against which a theological appraisal of Ishmael would be relevant:

> Abram continued: 'You have given me no children, and so my heir must be a slave born in my house'. Then came the word of the Lord to him: 'This man shall not be your heir; your heir shall be a child of your own body' (vv. 3-4).

These words reflect a very early fear over the procreativity of Abraham and the continued existence of his people. Once this danger

---

1. On Gen. 13 as Lot's elimination as heir to the covenant promise, cf. L.R. Helyer, 'The Separation of Abram and Lot: Its Significance in the Patriarchal Narratives', *JSOT* 26 (1983), pp. 77-88 (79-85).

had passed there arose another threat, that the memory of Abraham would be blotted out and he would no longer be venerated as the bearer of the divine promise (21.12-13). Israel had to face such threats on many occasions. In particular, it was a burning issue for the generation of the exiles and the postexilic community. Abraham's situation was their situation, and so it could make the promise to Abraham its own. The exile itself, as well as its prelude and aftermath, had shown that Israel was merely one tiny nation among a multitude of others (not least in Judah itself, with the peeling off of the governing Jewish stratum and the influx of foreign peoples). It would have seemed as though Israel were simply a plaything of other, mightier nations. The fact that Israel survived and returned to the land of Abraham was a sign that Yahweh was, after all, able to steer the course of history.

A Comparison with Deutero-Isaiah's Perspective on History

Deutero-Isaiah's view of history was wide enough to set these events in their true proportions as part of a total understanding of Israel's past. Yahweh was still the *régisseur* of the drama taking place in the days of the prophet, just as in primordial times (Isa. 42.5). Yahweh still held sway over foreign powers and their overlords. It was Yahweh who had taken Cyrus by the hand and led him to subdue nations and kings (Isa. 45.1). All his dealings with Cyrus were for the sake of Jacob-Israel (45.2), and surely this was proof enough that Yahweh was keeping his plans (46.10). Deutero-Isaiah was keenly aware that the exile had been a serious threat to Israel's belief in the validity of the promise to Abraham, but also that this threat was self-induced. The people of Israel were suffering for their disobedience of Yahweh's commandments and rejection of his prophets:

> If only you had listened to my commands, your prosperity would have rolled on like a river in flood and your righteousness like the waves of the sea; in number your offspring would have been like the sand and your descendants countless as its grains; their name would never have been erased or blotted out from my sight (Isa. 48.18-19; cf. Gen. 22.17; 13.16; 15.5).

The nations threatened to overwhelm Israel, and yet, paradoxically, it was only through the hand of foreigners that Israel could hope to be released from slavery in a foreign land. The turn of events would have appeared to be nothing more than a gigantic play of unknown and arbitrary forces, had not Yahweh been the faithful deliverer of Israel, constantly vigilant over its welfare.

Deutero-Isaiah's view of events provides the general background for understanding the 'Ishmael theology' of Genesis 17 and 21. The Priestly writers/redactors had to ponder the future of the holy people in the midst of the many foreign groups that surrounded them—some of whom, on crucial occasions, struggled for dominance over the whole region. This is clear from such texts as Ezra 4, which speaks of 'the peoples of the land' as the opponents of the returned exiles, and Neh. 2.19, which refers to specific individuals: 'Sanballat the Horonite, Tobiah the Ammonite slave and Geshem the Arab'. Likewise, the beginnings of the later conflict between Jews and Samaritans would certainly have been felt from an early period. Also, beyond the area of Jewish settlement (which in Nehemiah's time extended as far south as Beth-zur not far from Hebron, Neh. 3),[1] the region south of Judah had long since been inhabited by the Edomites/Idumaeans (against whom the Prophets raise their voice in anger, Ezek. 35.10-15; 36.5).[2]

The Inner-Jewish Conflict

The problem of foreign influence became acute in the period of the restoration. As S. Japhet has demonstrated, the many conflicts between the various strands within the Jewish community are given different emphases in different biblical books. Several groups identified themselves as 'the people of Israel' while adhering to different religious practices. The question of national identity became urgent.

> What should the relationship be between the people in the land of Israel and those outside it—or between the various communities within the land of Israel? How could the status of the diaspora within the concept 'Israel' be determined—would it apply to all these communities, any part of them, or none? In short: who is 'Israel'?[3]

---

1. Cf. also E. Schürer, *The History of the Jewish People in the Age of Jesus Christ (175 BC–AD 135)*, II (Edinburgh: T. & T. Clark, rev. edn, 1979), p. 2 n. 4; S. Japhet, 'People and Land in the Restoration Period', in G. Strecker (ed.), *Das Land Israel in biblischer Zeit* (Jerusalem Symposium 1981 der Hebräischen Universität und der Georg-August-Universität; Göttinger Theologische Arbeiten, 25; Göttingen: Vandenhoeck & Ruprecht, 1983), pp. 103-25 (114).

2. Cf. further below on Edom; in late biblical times, they were subjugated and forcibly converted to Judaism.

3. Cf. Japhet, 'People and Land', p. 106.

Such issues are reflected in texts such as Ezek. 33.23-24, which refers to 'the inhabitants of these waste places in the land of Israel', who say, 'Abraham was only one man, yet he got possession of the land; but we are many; the land is surely given to us to possess'. This is the claim that was raised by those who remained in Judah against the exiles in Babylonia,[1] and their argument of a *a minore ad maius* type (Abraham—one; we—many) was backed up by their allegation against the exiles, 'you have gone far from the Lord' (Ezek. 11.15).

But the Jews of the exile could also appeal to the promise to Abraham:

> But you, Israel, my servant, Jacob whom I have chosen, the offspring of Abraham, my friend; you whom I took from the ends of the earth and called from its farthest corners (Isa. 41.8-9).

The 'offspring of Abraham' here is clearly those scattered among the nations who will be gathered back to the land of Israel[2] (compare Ezek. 11.16-17). Isa. 51.1-2 also probably represents a reaction against the attitude shown in Ezek. 33.24:

> For when he [Abraham] was but one I called him, and I blessed him and made him many (Isa. 51.2).

The books of Ezra–Nehemiah show a more radical and strongly religious view. There is and can be only one Israelite nation: the returned exiles. The others are foreigners, 'peoples of the land'. As will be seen below, Ezra's uncompromising attitude towards mixed marriages reveals an intense religious zeal for the purity of the nation. Clearly, the question of who had the right to claim identity with 'the seed of Abraham' was hotly disputed between the various groups within the Jewish community.

The Foreign Presence and National Unity

In addition to the internal conflict over who were the true 'sons of Abraham', the Jewish nation had also to come to terms with the presence of foreigners in the land promised to Abraham. The problem was not totally new, since individual foreigners had been allowed into Israel (2 Sam. 15.17-22) and had enjoyed a certain amount of protection.

---

1. Cf. Japhet, 'People and Land', pp. 106-107.
2. Cf. Japhet, 'People and Land', pp. 108-109, and on the following, pp. 109-16.

They could even be 'adopted' by circumcision and thereby be allowed to take part in the Passover celebrations. This tolerance lived on:

> [The Passover-lamb] was eaten by the people of Israel who had returned from exile, and also by every one who had [joined them and][1] separated himself from the pollutions of the peoples of the land to worship the Lord, the God of Israel (Ezra 6.21; cf. Neh. 10.29).

Japhet identifies 'those who had joined them . . . ' with converts to the Judaism of the period. Isa. 56.3-8 displays a similar openness to foreigners prevalent in the period shortly after the return:

> Let not the foreigner who has joined himself to the Lord say, 'The Lord will surely separate me from his people'. . . And the foreigners who join themselves to the Lord, to minister to him, to love the name of the Lord, and to be his servants, every one who keeps the sabbath, and does not profane it, and holds fast my covenant—these I will bring to my holy mountain, and make them joyful in my house of prayer; their burnt offerings and their sacrifices will be accepted on my altar; for my house shall be called a house of prayer for all peoples (Isa. 56.3, 6-7).

The number of these 'converts' must have been quite considerable if such a program of minimum requirements for their acceptance had to be worked out. However, the very fact that the foreigner feared being 'cut off' (*hiph.* of *bdl*) from the community suggests that that was also a possibility; and even though individual proselytes were welcomed, the Jewish community—a minority in its 'own' land—could hardly afford a policy of welcoming 'foreigners' *en masse*.

In the interest of religious and national unity, some line between Jew and non-Jew will have been perceived as necessary to draw; and for this, Ishmael's case could be used as a model. Yahweh had made a clear distinction between Ishmael and Isaac:

> As for Ishmael, I have heard you; behold, I will bless him and make him fruitful and multiply him exceedingly; he shall be the father of twelve princes, and I will make him a great nation. But I will establish my covenant with Isaac, whom Sarah shall bear to you at this season next year (Gen. 17.20).

Upholding the covenant took precedence over generosity towards Ishmael.

---

1. On *nibdāl min-'al*, cf. Japhet, 'People and Land', p. 117.

In a postexilic context this meant safeguarding Jewish religious institutions (including marriage) against foreign influence. In the books of Ezra–Nehemiah this lent an almost ritualistic flavour to the act of *separation*. The presence of foreigner was thought to bring 'pollution' and 'guilt' upon the land, for which 'atonement' had to be made. A case in point is the handling of intermarriages in Ezra.[1] The problem is judged primarily on religious grounds, and it is on religious grounds that Malachi, Nehemiah and Ezra exhibit a similar attitude towards foreign wives; compare Mal. 2.11:

> Judah has violated the holiness of Yahweh which he loves and married daughters of an alien god.

According to v. 12 the abomination will be ended by cutting off 'every man who does this' from Israel, which evidently implies the banishment of the offending husbands. According to Ezra 9.11-12, the religious principle of holiness requires that the land be purified from the pollution of foreign wives[2] (carried out in Ezra 10), a situation which was in flagrant infringement of the solemn vow in Neh. 10.30.

The violation of the land by foreigners in Ezra is a clear reference to the laws concerning heathen pollution and its purification in Lev. 18.24-25, and also to the Deuteronomic law of *ḥērem* and the purity of the assembly (Deut. 7.1-3; compare Neh. 13.1). These laws required that all heathen abominations be banished because they had polluted the land. The terms used—*bdl hiph.* in Ezra 10.11 (Neh. 13.3; cf. also Isa. 56.3 quoted above)[3] and *yṣ' hiph.* (Ezra 10.3.19)—can be compared to the corresponding verbs in Lev. 18.24: *šlḥ* (*piel*, 'send away') and *qy'* ('vomit', 18.25, 28); cf. Deut. 7.16 (*'kl*, 'consume') and Mal. 2.12 (*krt*, 'cut off').

---

1. Smith (*The Religion of the Landless*, p. 82) refers to the low position of women in Yemeni Jewish society—the women were potentially dangerous sources of influence from the outside; cf. also p. 145.

2. Cf. A.H.J. Gunneweg, *Esra: Mit einer Zeittafel von Alfred Jepsen* (KAT, 19/1; Gütersloh: Mohn, 1985), pp. 161-63.

3. Cf. E. Schwarz, *Identität durch Abgrenzung: Abgrenzungsprozesse in Israel im 2. vorchristlichen Jahrhundert und ihre traditionsgeschichtlichen Voraussetzungen: Zugleich ein Beitrag zur Erforschung des Jubiläenbuches* (Europäische Hochschulschriften, Reihe XXIII, Theologie, 162; Frankfurt a.M.: Peter Lang, 1982), pp. 63-66 (in Schwarz's perception, Ezra 9–10 achieves its climax in 10.11). In P-usage, *bdl* seems to serve to categorize between Israelites and foreigners; cf. Smith, *The Religion of the Landless*, p. 148.

For the postexilic assembly, these laws were translated into their situation as the divorce and expulsion of their own foreign wives. There seem to have been two models for this.

a. *The Day of Atonement.* Sending off foreign wives removed the 'guilt' from Israel. The gathering in Jerusalem in Ezra 10 may be described deliberately to suggest a ritual like the Day of Atonement, in which Israel's guilt is driven away into the desert with the scape-goat (Lev. 16). Likewise, in Ezra 10, the guilt is physically removed when the women depart from Israel.

b. *The Expulsion of Hagar.* Abraham's sending away of Hagar and Ishmael could also have been appealed to as a model. *šlḥ* (*piel*) is frequently used in the sense 'divorce a wife' (Deut. 21.14; 22.19, 29; Jer. 3.8; 1 Chron. 8.8) and the same verb, *wyšlḥh*, is used for the expulsion of Hagar in Gen. 21.14. Just as Solomon, whose foreign wives led to his corruption, had set the bad example (Neh. 13.25-26; cf. Exod. 34.16), so Abraham's treatment of Hagar the Egyptian could be regarded as the correct model.[1] According to the MT of Ezra 10.44, some of the foreign wives had children. Unfortunately, the text as it now stands (obviously corrupted by dittography) does not make it clear whether these children were also expelled together with their mothers. The Septuagint implies that both children and wives alike were sent away (1 Esd. 9.36: καὶ ἀπέλυσαν αὐτὰς σὺν τέκνοις),[2] in a clear parallel to the fate of Hagar and Ishmael. If this were true of the MT as well, then God's advice to Abraham, 'Cast out this slave woman with her son' (Gen. 21.10), would have found a literal application in the nationalistic program of Ezra 9–10.

I conclude that the *Sitz im Leben* of an 'Ishmael theology' would have been the struggles of the Jewish community soon after the exile. This theology would have informed the decisions that had to be taken on how to preserve the Jewish nation under the covenant of Abraham (Neh. 9.7). These decisions are exemplified by the theological program of the book of Ezra, although the program described in ch. 10 may reflect the author's own convictions and ideals more than any practical solution.[3] This undoubtedly had its root in the crucial

---

1. That Abraham had much earlier become the model of trust and hope can be inferred from Isa. 29.22; 41.8; 51.2; Ezek. 33.24.

2. Cf. also Gunneweg, *Esra*, p. 184.

3. Cf. Gunneweg, *Esra*, pp. 162, 172-75. Gunneweg points out the dependence of Ezra 9.12 on Neh. 13.25: what in Neh. is an individual case, becomes in

question of Israel's survival amidst foreign nations.[1] In this situation guidance could be gained from God's former dealings with Israel and the patriarchs. In the days of the rise of the Persian Empire, Deutero-Isaiah had opened the eyes of the exiles to the full scope of the salvation-history, claiming that they were witnessing no less than a repetition of God's miraculous acts of the past. The Priestly writers, as is clear from the P material in the Pentateuch, took more interest in 'halachic' applications of the 'letter of the law', particularly to the question of how to reconcile the limits of the covenant with the presence of foreigners among the chosen people. Obviously a literal adherence to the biblical command to 'blot out' the foreign peoples was out of the question, but these foreign peoples had at least to be kept at bay. The holy nation had still to be kept holy to prove worthy of being chosen by God 'out of all the peoples that are on the face on the earth' (Deut. 7.6).[2] On that basis, it is also understandable that the Priestly writers should have taken a keen interest in the organization of the different peoples of the earth, as witnessed by the genealogies and tables of nations (e.g. Gen. 25). The 'Ishmael theology' offered a way of understanding why God had favoured certain nations. (Compare this with the Rabbinic haggadah in which God first offers the Torah to several nations, including the Ishmaelites, before it is finally accepted by Israel.)[3]

There is a danger in placing too much reliance on the historical value of the material in Ezra. Vink dismisses Ezra 9–10 as irrelevant for outlining the mission and character of Ezra the *priest*. He finds the two chapters to be legendary; they only attest to the exclusiveness and rigorism of the Jewish minority of the Maccabean era. But Vink does take notice of the fact that Neh. 13.23-25, although not prescribing such drastic and far-reaching measures as the two Ezra chapters, nevertheless demonstrates a similar rigorism.[4] J.M. Myers thinks that these verses testify to the threat posed by intermarriage against the whole character of the postexilic community in the time of Nehemiah.[5]

Ezra 9–10 an affair for the whole community under Ezra himself.
    1. Cf. Gunneweg, *Esra*, pp. 171-72.
    2. Cf. also Japhet, 'People and Land', p. 114.
    3. On the story as it appears in the (Palestinian) Targums on Deut. 33.2 and elsewhere, cf. Syrén, *The Blessings*, pp. 144-48.
    4. Vink, 'The Date and Origin', pp. 30-32.
    5. Cf. J.M. Myers, *Ezra, Nehemiah: Introduction, Translation, and Notes* (AB;

Vink's thesis of a Maccabean date for Ezra 9–10 is strong, but Rudolph's case, on the basis of chs. 7–10, that Ezra himself, rather than the Chronicler, was primarily responsible for the Ezra report (*die Ezra-Erzählung*) is a good one.[1] A compromise would be to view Ezra 9–10 as presenting a programmatic ideal—regardless of whether it was ever put into effect. In this way Rudolph links the measures taken in Ezra 9–11 to the activities of Ezra himself.[2]

My view is that the question of historicity is not essential for an overall understanding of Ezra 9–10. The situation addressed there is perhaps more rhetorical than historical, but to the author of these chapters it was nonetheless very 'real'. Regardless of their precise historical value, the chapters give a feel for the atmosphere in a period at some distance in time from the exile. The very existence of the chapters referred to in Ezra–Nehemiah, as well as Gen. 17.19-21, testifies to the anxiety prevailing in Priestly circles for the continuation of the Israelite nation. This anxiety expressed itself in a two ways: in a keen interest in the validity of the covenant (Gen. 17), and in an assiduous concern for the purity of the people (Ezra–Nehemiah).

Vink also differs from me in his interpretation of Genesis 17. He discerns in it a non-nationalistic, universalistic outlook inherent in P's view of sacred history and the Law. He sees this universalism as very inclusive. The emphasis on the covenant with Abraham was linked to his ethnic origin; Abraham has become the symbol of the Jewish race as it spread all over the Near East. Like that of Noah, the covenant of Abraham is unlimited in space and time.[3] However, Vink's interpretation of Genesis 17 does not take proper account of the hesitation, even reservation, over an outright universalism implied in the text. The covenant with Abraham in Gen. 17.20-21 will apply to Isaac alone; Ishmael will have no part in it. There is surely a clear demarcation between those who are included in the covenant and those who are

---

New York: Doubleday, 1965), p. 216; also W. Rudolph, *Esra und Nehemia samt 3. Esra* (HAT, 20; Tübingen: Mohr, 1930), p. 208.

1. Cf. Rudolph, *Esra und Nehemia*, pp. 100-103.

2. Cf. Rudolph, *Esra und Nehemia*, pp. 85-87. Note also the root *'rb* in both Ezra 9.12 and Neh. 13.3.

3. Cf. Vink, 'The Date and Origin', pp. 90-91. Blum (*Vätergeschichte*, pp. 457-58) examines how the interplay between history and contemporary context (the conflict between Judah and Samaria) may have affected the transmission of the P material.

not; not even all of Abraham's children are children of the covenant. Chapter 17 certainly testifies to a universalistic outlook, but that outlook is not 'unlimited'; a special place is reserved for Israel among the nations of the world. There were indeed 'many' and 'great' nations around and even *within* Israel. Some of these could be reckoned as Abraham's children, but that did not mean that they were all partakers of the one, holy covenant.

Summary

There is, it is true, no direct evidence in the sources that an 'Ishmael theology' existed. No appeal is made to Abraham's treatment of Hagar and Ishmael. Nonetheless, Abraham's expulsion of Hagar and Ishmael serves as a rhetorical example for resolving the issue of national purity. The integrity of the land, religion and people—all had to be protected. According to sacred tradition, God had not rejected Ishmael altogether. He was Abraham's offspring and one of the circumcised. In principle, Ishmael had a certain standing in matters of religion and community life in general. His case could be taken as a precedent for a generous attitude towards foreigners who wished to be circumcised and join in the festivals such as Passover. But Ishmael could not expect a share in the covenant by virtue of birth alone; his people were not 'holy' in the sense that Israel was ('a priestly nation'). His position had to be specially regulated by God.

If this seems paradoxical, it is only because Ishmael remains a paradoxical figure: tolerated and not tolerated; cast out, but not totally. Gen. 17.19-21 represents a genuine attempt to clarify the postexilic situation and to moderate the impact of harshly conflicting views on the different claims to the legacy of Abraham. Following the example of Abraham, true Israelites could not accept the presence of foreigners in their homes and families, even as wives. But at the same time, by giving Ishmael to Abraham and by blessing the son's future, God had shown that there was a place in his plans for the 'peoples of the land', who by birth (as in the case of non-exiled Jews) or conversion could ask to be accepted into the community.

Chapter 3

THE ESAU TEXTS

The Esau texts fall into two groups. The first covers the major features
of his life: his birth and adolescence, where he lived, and his marriages and genealogy. Mention of his death is conspiciously lacking.
After his departure from Jacob, Esau vanishes into the unknown. The
texts of the second group are concerned with the relationship with his
brother Jacob, his father Isaac and his mother Rebecca. Among these
are the narratives in which Esau loses his birthright and his father's
blessing. The theme of the separation from and reunion with Jacob
also figures prominently.

Esau's whole life is marked by the relationship with his twin
brother, which is mainly one of competition and conflict. The information given in the first group of texts seems merely to fill in the gaps
between the larger narratives. The brothers have already competed
for superiority in their mother's womb, and from birth they exhibit
totally opposite natures (Gen. 25 and 27). On occasion Esau's conduct
is a direct reaction to a preceding action by Jacob. So, for example,
when Jacob attempts to obtain a wife from his own stock, Esau goes and
marries Mahalath, daughter of Ishmael (Gen. 28.6). Esau's settlement
in Seir is seen in Gen. 33.16 and 36.6-8 as consequent upon his departure from Jacob. Only his first marriages (26.34) happen without any
reference to his brother. Even so, it is these first wives that encourage
Rebecca to send Jacob away to seek a mate from her own family:

> I am weary of my life because of the Hittite women. If Jacob marries one
> of the Hittite women such as these, one of the women of the land, what
> good will my life be to me? (Gen. 27.46).

In short, the dominant motif in the Jacob–Esau cycle is the sequence
conflict–separation/departure. The departure may take the form of
flight (Jacob to Laban) or it may be voluntary. The cause of the
voluntary departure in 36.7 is, as in the case of Abraham and Lot, the

inability of the land to sustain both Jacob's and Esau's cattle (the wording of 36.7 seems to be copied from 13.6). On the other hand, in 33.12-16 the motive is part of Jacob's strategy for avoiding open warfare, which is also the guiding principle for Abraham in 13.8.

As Skinner has pointed out,[1] the texts portray Esau in two different ways. In chs. 25 and 27 he is 'the rude natural man' who despises his birthright, lives by his sword and bears a grudge against his brother. In ch. 33, by contrast, he behaves like a noble *sheikh* in charge of a clan and is only too eager to reach an accommodation with Jacob. Or, as T.L. Thompson puts it, 'By the time that Jacob has stayed with Laban..., Esau has become a people'.[2] The relationship between Jacob and Esau is now totally transformed. In 33.4 Esau is greeted as Jacob's equal, or, rather, as his superior.

Earlier, in Genesis 25 and 27, they are repeatedly contrasted. Chapter 25.27-34 describes their differences: they are of different appearance and character; they choose different walks of life; they are even preferred by different parents.[3] These differences and contrasts unfold further in ch. 27: 'hairy' and 'smooth' in 27.11; voice and hands in 27.22. It does not take much imagination to detect behind the stories about Jacob and Esau a pattern of oppositions such as 'dark–light', 'hard–soft', even 'male–female'. Categorizing by opposites appears elsewhere in the Bible—beginning with the Creation story in Genesis 1—and this motif may well have been an important principle in compiling the original stories.[4]

Various literary devices can be detected throughout the Jacob–Esau complex, and, for that matter, throughout the entire Jacob Cycle. The

1. Skinner, *Genesis*, p. 415.
2. T.L. Thompson, 'Conflict Themes in the Jacob Narratives', *Semeia* 15 (1979), pp. 5-26 (17-18).
3. Cf. M. Fishbane, 'Composition and Structure in the Jacob Cycle', *JJS* 26 (1975), pp. 15-38 (21); Cf. *idem, Text and Texture: Close Readings of Selected Biblical Texts* (The Schocken Jewish Bookshelf; New York: Schocken Books, 1979), pp. 40-62; Blum, *Vätergeschichte*, p. 185.
4. Cf. Levi-Strauss's idea of folk tales and myths as systems of binary oppositions that reveal tensions and dialectics unique to a given culture. For his impact on Old Testament study, cf. J.W. Rogerson, *Myth in Old Testament Interpretation* (BZAW, 134; Berlin: de Gruyter, 1974), pp. 101-105. Fishbane ('Composition and Structure', p. 35) argues along similar lines when he finds three such binary polarities throughout the whole Jacob Cycle: barrenness and fertility; curse and blessing; profane space/exile and sacred space/homeland.

'leading motifs' in these complexes have been variously identified by different scholars. Thompson[1] considers the theme of *conflict* between various characters to be a principal motif. R. Alter has coined the term 'narrative analogy' for the repetion of a similar theme in various contexts.[2] P.D. Miscall points to three instances of general analogy between the Jacob and Joseph stories: deception of the father and treachery between brothers, separation from the younger brother, and eventual reunion and reconciliation between estranged brothers.[3] Instances of 'narrative analogy' can also be found *within* the Jacob Cycle itself, and even within its constitutive parts such as the Jacob–Esau complex.

The figure of Esau cries out for comparison with Ishmael.[4] The two 'outsiders' have much in common, and a formal bond between them is established by the alliance between Esau and Ishmael's daughter. Each has a significant relationship with a younger brother that ends in separation. The father takes a favourable attitude towards the elder (see Gen. 17.18 and 21.11 for Abraham–Ishmael, and 25.28 for Isaac–Esau), and the mother favours the younger. Sarah regards Ishmael as a threat to the welfare of Isaac (21.10), and Rebecca reacts to a threat against Jacob from Esau's side (27.42). Only the solution is different in each case. In Genesis 28 it is Jacob who flees to Laban, while Esau stays at home, whereas in Genesis 21 it is the younger brother who remains, while the elder is forced to leave. In this particular case, the reversal of roles may represent a deliberate variation of the narrative analogy.[5] Further similarities between the stories of Ishmael and Esau can be seen in the pre-natal oracles received by their mothers (16.11; 25.23) and the crucial episode of thirst/starvation (21.16; 25.30).

There are also significant differences between the stories of Ishmael

1. Thompson, 'Conflict Themes in the Jacob Narratives', pp. 5-8; cf. *idem, The Origin Tradition of Ancient Israel. I. The Literary Formation of Genesis and Exodus 1–23* (JSOTSup, 55; Sheffield: JSOT Press, 1987), pp. 104, 110.

2. Cf. 'A Literary Approach to the Bible', *Commentary* 60 (1975), pp. 70-77 (73); cf. also references in P.D. Miscall, 'The Jacob and Joseph Stories as Analogies', *JSOT* 6 (1978), pp. 28-40 (28, 39).

3. Cf. Miscall, 'The Jacob and Joseph Stories as Analogies', pp. 31-32.

4. For other analogies within the Old Testament, cf. Miscall, 'The Jacob and Joseph Stories as Analogies', pp. 29-30. A comprehensive survey of intersecting representations of Esau/Edom and Ishmael in Genesis is given by Dicou, *Jakob en Esau*, pp. 54-55.

5. On 'variation in repetition', see Alter, *The Art of Biblical Narrative*, p. 100.

and Esau that must not be overlooked. The most obvious of these is the difference in their genealogical status: Jacob and Esau are twins; Ishmael and Isaac are only half-brothers. Another conspicuous difference is simply the quantity of narrative that concerns them. I have already remarked how little information there is on Ishmael in the biblical sources. By comparison, Esau is much more of a 'personality', simply because we are told much more about him. He also plays a much more active role in the narrative. He speaks, he acts, he prepares food and introduces himself to Isaac as his first-born. In threatening Jacob with revenge (27.41), he resembles Cain more than Ishmael. His conflict with Jacob is different in that it is a more truly fraternal conflict than in the case of Ishmael and Isaac. By and large, compared to the Ishmael sections, the Esau–Jacob narrative is more elaborate, with various digressions and developments. However, the Esau sections do lack a parallel to Genesis 17: the promise to Ishmael of many descendants.

Evidently Esau was not as 'useful', from a theological perspective, as was Ishmael. This is probably related to the fact that, as pointed out by Westermann and others before him,[1] a theologically conceived promise has no determining function in Gen. 25.19–36.43 (except in the prayer of Jacob 32.12). Moreover, given the equation of Esau with Edom (see below), reassurance of the continued existence for Esau was redundant!

A Review of Scholarly Opinions on the Jacob–Esau Complex

'Traditional' versus 'Modern' Approaches

In the scholarly treatment of the Jacob–Esau complex, it is necessary nowadays to differentiate between the traditional approach and a new trend. By 'traditional approach' I mean the established historical methods, such as observations on the various Pentateuchal sources, and form-critical considerations about saga material and its antecedents. The 'new trend', markedly literary in its orientation, has already been represented in the introduction to this section by the names Fishbane and Thompson. The Jacob story has turned out to be very popular with this new school.[2] Representatives of this new trend seldom turn

1. Cf. Westermann, *Genesis 12–36*, p. 499.
2. Apart from those names referred to here and below, for whom the Jacob Cycle forms a substantial part of their material, S. Bar-Efrat (*Narrative Art in the*

to the classical methods (including those of Gunkel), and tend to regard them as outdated.[1] In other words, the 'new' approach aims at a methodological shift away from diachronic questions of original shape, antecedent traditions and the like. Instead, the focus is on structural unity and on a synchronic analysis that also draws on modern study of folklore. Although Fishbane himself considers questions of historical actuality in texts such as Gen. 25.23 and 27.40, he criticizes the traditional methods for their tendency to regard the Patriarchal narratives as mirroring actual historical and sociological conditions in early Israel.[2] He also criticizes the inclination to explain such things as narrative repetitions and stylistic variations by pointing to an original diversity of sources.[3] Instead, the texts should be treated as primarily fictional, literary works of art, exhibiting 'symmetrical coherence'.[4]

The new approach is in many respects commendable, since it opens up new dimensions of the text that were previously disregarded or only vaguely apprehended. The move away from an insistence on imposing points of dating and matters of historical and sociological concern extrinsic to the biblical texts and towards a greater respect for their intrinsic qualities *qua* texts should be rewarding.[5] As the case of theories about the Israelite invasion of Canaan shows, the function of the biblical documents as historical evidence is being pushed more and more into the background.[6] M. Sternberg, in his imposing work,

Bible) and M. Sternberg (*The Poetics of Biblical Narrative*) must be mentioned for their similar approach. Dicou (*Jakob en Esau*) also deals with the Jacob–Esau complex from synchronic aspects (cf. pp. 3-4) and compares the portrait of Esau in Genesis to that in the prophetic books.

1. Cf. Fishbane, 'Composition and Structure', p. 18. Cf. also Thompson's criticism of what he terms 'the received opinion', in 'Conflict Themes in the Jacob Narratives', p. 8. He confesses in that article to having himself been over-influenced by this 'received opinion' in his *The Historicity of the Patriarchal Narratives: The Quest for the Historical Abraham* (BZAW, 133; Berlin: de Gruyter, 1974).

2. Cf. especially Thompson, 'Conflict Themes in the Jacob Narratives', pp. 8, 115.

3. M. Fishbane, 'Composition and Structure'; Fokkelman, *Narrative Art in Genesis*, pp. 2-4.

4. Fishbane, 'Composition and Structure', pp. 21-22; Miscall, 'The Jacob and Joseph Stories as Analogies', pp. 28-30.

5. Cf. the opening pages in Fokkelman, *Narrative Art in Genesis*.

6. Cf. especially N.P. Lemche, 'Rachel and Leah: Or: On the Survival of Outdated Paradigms in the Study of the Origin of Israel II', *SJOT* (1988), pp. 39-65 (53-55).

The Poetics of Biblical Narrative, takes a very decided view on what does and does not constitute a 'literary' study of the Bible. He disdains being associated with 'the literary approach'[1] and does not abandon the historical dimension of biblical studies. To him, the study of the historical milieu, world view and the formation of the tradition are all indispensable to literary study;[2] but he shares the belief in the 'futility' of traditional source criticism. Although 'source-oriented' inquiry and 'discourse-oriented' analysis do not focus on the same questions, they must both be taken seriously.[3] Biblical narrative evolved as a complex, multifunctional discourse regulated by three principles: ideological (e.g. 'law'), historiographic (e.g. dates, names, places) and aesthetic (motivation, dialogue, interior speech and the like). These three regulating principles merge into a single 'poetics' in 'reading as a drama'.[4] Sternberg also addresses questions of multiple authorship, although he stresses the principle of biblical 'unity in variety'.[5]

The strength of the 'literary' method is that it is a hermeneutical tool that offers a new way of understanding texts as *texts*. On the other hand, some of its effects may run counter to a full understanding of the texts as *biblical* texts. Westermann maintains that the synchronic approach does not exclude the earlier methods with their discrimination between different layers in order to reach the 'original' unit. In defence of a similar persistence on my part, two arguments may be raised:

1. In practice, a treatment such as that of Fishbane and Thompson of the Jacob–stories seems to leave a very narrow range of possibilities for an ideal 'best' explanation.[6] It leaves unanswered such questions as when and how the text came into being and the identity of the author. Although in 'the literary approach' the author is given a very prominent position as

1. *The Poetics*, pp. 2-5; on his objections against what he terms 'the New Criticism', cf. 7-10 (he does not mention the names to which I have referred).
2. Cf. *The Poetics*, p. 13.
3. Cf. *The Poetics*, pp. 15-16, 22.
4. Cf. *The Poetics*, pp. 41, 46.
5. Cf. *The Poetics*, pp. 71, 73-75.
6. Cf. the excellent article by S. Boorer, 'The Importance of a Diachronic Approach: The Case of Genesis–Kings', *CBQ* 51 (1989), pp. 195-208 (195-96: 205). She argues that a consideration of the diachronic dimension of a text is an important component of any interpretation of the present biblical text.

the 'artist',[1] little is said about the actual point at which the author enters the process of the text's formation—was it at the oral, written or redactional stage? Is the 'artist' identical with the last 'redactor'? Questions about contradictions in biblical texts tend to receive *ad hoc* answers that do not effectively account for the diversity of lengthy biblical passages.

2. The 'literary approach' owes much to methods of structural analysis that have been worked out on the basis of modern literary texts by one (known) author. Is such a single-author perspective going to give the best results if applied to Old Testament texts? On the other hand, if folkloristic literature from other cultures is used for comparison, then the importance of the individual personalities[2] of the biblical history is missed.[3]

Fokkelman and Fishbane do, it must be said, place the Jacob Cycle within a wider Old Testament frame, and this has theological implications. Fokkelman proposes two frames of reference. One is formal: the family history that covers most of Genesis and which is at the same time a national history. The other is theological: it is God's 'blessing' that sets this history going, starting with Abraham, and ensures its continuation from generation to generation—so much so that the power to generate is itself only possible thanks to the 'blessing'. From this double perspective Fokkelman can explain why Genesis came to include so many genealogies. On one hand, they are intended to complete the picture of each generation before the next one begins. On the other, the genealogies demonstrate the efficacy of God's blessing. The blessing works in manifold ways throughout Genesis, and in all these works God is the decisive agent. God is the one who acts and blesses. In this way, the Jacob Cycle can also be seen as part of the larger whole, the history of salvation.[4] Interestingly,

1. Cf. Fokkelman, *Narrative Art in Genesis*, pp. 5-6. As early as 1922 Gunkel had spoken of 'die Kunstform' of the sagas in Genesis; cf. Gunkel, *Genesis*, p. xxvii.
2. Cf. Sternberg, *Poetics*, pp. 329-30.
3. A. Berlin (*Poetics and Interpretation of Biblical Narrative* [Bible and Literature Series, 9; Sheffield: Almond Press, 1983], p. 19), in a similar vein, stresses that biblical narrative needs a theoretical basis worked out on its own premises, not one imported from some alien corpus of texts.
4. Cf. Fokkelman, *Narrative Art in Genesis*, pp. 239-40.

Esau's role within this scheme is limited to the family-historical frame of reference. Even if he is a 'loose end', he is nonetheless needed to complete the picture of his generation. He is still a descendant of Isaac and Abraham.[1] Yet he has no apparent theological role to play. Because of this Fokkelman does not mention him within the theological frames of blessing and salvation.

Fishbane also takes 'blessing', together with 'birth' and 'land' (or 'inheritance'),[2] as the three main elements underlying the text. 'Birth', 'blessing' and 'land' together constitute the divine promise to Abraham. Each of these motifs has its own opposing element, and therefore they reflect the hopes of an ancient Israelite culture, just as their opposites reflect its anxieties. God's election of Israel is actualized in them and realized in the success of individual humans.[3]

It cannot be denied that these are deep insights into the Jacob story. What one may doubt is whether these insights depend on the particular method practiced by Fokkelman and Fishbane.

Yet another approach, a sort of middle ground between the traditional schools and the innovative course taken by Fokkelman and others (although definitely more on the 'traditional' side) is taken by E. Blum in his *Die Komposition der Vätergeschichte* (1984). Although he occasionally uses terms from source criticism (e.g. D for Gen. 32.10-13; see below), Blum regularly rejects a multi-source explanation of a passage in favour of seeing it as a consistent unit. The logical outcome of this is that the Jacob story constitutes one self-sufficient ('in sich ruhende') and independent complex of tradition.[4] Within the 'larger' units, there are only revised strata, the D stratum and the Priestly stratum (the *'D'-Bearbeitung* and the *priesterliche Schicht*).[5] It is only fair, then, that Blum should commend R. Rendtorff's methodological reappraisal of the formation of the Pentateuch.[6] Blum

1. Cf. Fokkelman, *Narrative Art in Genesis*, p. 239.
2. Cf. Fishbane, 'Composition and Structure', p. 35.
3. Cf. Fishbane, *Text and Texture*, p. 62.
4. Cf. Blum, *Vätergeschichte*, p. 150.
5. Cf. Blum, *Vätergeschichte*, pp. 362, 420.
6. Cf. Blum, *Vätergeschichte*, p. 466. On Rendtorff's 'larger units', cf. his *Das Überlieferungsgeschichtliche Problem des Pentateuch* (BZAW, 147; Berlin: de Gruyter, 1977), pp. 151-53. Another apparent influence on Blum would be H. Eising, *Formgeschichtliche Untersuchung zur Jakobserzählung der Genesis* (Emsdetten: Lechte, 1940), cf. pp. 160-61, 444-45, whose steadfast assertion of the unity of the Jacob–Esau–Laban complex from form-historical considerations is

The Forsaken First-Born

is very sceptical about attempts to trace any pre-Israelite basis for the patriarchal stories, and likewise he repudiates the hypothesis that the patriarchal traditions are cult-traditions (Noth; also Alt's *Väterreligion*) or family stories (Westermann).[1]

But although Blum holds that the Jacob story forms one unit, he does not believe that it was created in one piece. On the contrary, it has a complex history of transmission. There were certain 'building stones' on which the later composition (*Kompositionsschicht*) and narration were constructed.[2] One such 'building stone' was the Jacob–Esau–Laban tradition which is in turn split up into a 'Jakob–Esau Überlieferung' and a 'Jakob–Laban Überlieferung'.[3] The Jacob–Esau stories in Genesis 25 and 27 are of a southern provenience where Israel/Judah and Esau/Edom lay adjacent to each other. Indeed, Gen. 25.23b, 27.29a (37a) and 40a are clear allusions to the submission of Edom under David. The historical context of the Jacob–Esau stories in chs. 25 and 27 is the time of the united monarchy, as can be deduced from 25.29 and 27.37, which presume that the Israelite state is a great power in Syria-Palestine. The sagas understand the patriarchs as ancestors of peoples: Israel, Edom and Aram (Laban). But it is not a question of nationalized cultural myths or dramatized tribal history. Rather, they are 'episodes' from the early history of Israel and its neighbours that are connected with the world of the narrator by means of etiological construction. However, the Jacob story as a whole originated in the North in the time of Jeroboam I. Among the arguments for this are the toponyms of the 'Kompositionsschicht'—which are all found in the North—and the particular role given to Joseph among the children of Jacob. Blum connects the original Jacob story with king Jeroboam's endeavours to consolidate his position after the debacle of the united kingdom. Read in this way, the Jacob story can be understood as a program by which the political and religious innovations under Jeroboam are read back into Israel's beginnings

impressive. He sees in 25.19–28.9 and 32.2–33.16 a bisected frame-narrative (*Rahmenerzählung*) around the Jacob–Laban story. Unevenness and oddities are seen as manifestations of his manner and style rather than indications of cracks in the literary structure. Furthermore, the Jacob story was worked out on the basis of much pre-existent *written* material.

    1.   Cf. Blum, *Vätergeschichte*, pp. 491, 501.
    2.   Cf. Blum, *Vätergeschichte*, pp. 168-71; 202-203.
    3.   Cf. Blum, *Vätergeschichte*, pp. 190-95, and on the following, pp. 195-202.

and given the authority of Jacob the Patriarch.

The success of Blum's work is that it places the Jacob story at one particular point in Israel's history and at the same time explains its individual elements. So saying, I cannot endorse all his results. In my view, his explanation of chs. 32–33 as reflecting a northern Israelite antipathy against a southern imperialism is not entirely successful (cf. further below).

Thompson also suggests that large narrative units (five or six) form the basis of Genesis and Exodus 1–23. These units, designated 'traditional complex-chain narratives', represent an ancient narrative genre, both *literary and oral*. The Jacob–Esau complex formed one such unit, and is the longest narrative unit taken into the 'Toledoth of Isaac'.[1] It is constructed of a tripartite introduction in ch. 25 and an extended 'plot-line of conflict' that ends finally in 33.15-17.[2]

My survey of both 'traditional' and 'modern' approaches demonstrates one thing at least: that there is no lack of scholarly willingness to reconsider old positions and see new aspects of these much read and admired passages.[3] They show a fundamentally sound inquisitive attitude to the biblical material and a similarly sound readiness to challenge earlier standard opinions. What I will try to do here is not to give precedence to any particular approach, but to be as eclectic as possible in considering how the material may best be understood. Accordingly, I shall neglect neither the study of the origins of the texts, however hypothetical its results may look to some,[4] nor observations on the structure and literary character of the textual units as we have them. As in the previous section, my approach here will be first to look into matters concerning the form and structure of the texts before considering the question of origins,[5] including a survey of the shifting views within the 'traditional' schools.

---

1. Cf. Thompson, *The Origin Tradition of Ancient Israel*, pp. 156-57, 161.

2. Cf. Thompson, *The Origin Tradition of Ancient Israel*, pp. 111, 161.

3. Yet another course is taken by Blank ('Studies in Post-Exilic Universalism', pp. 159-60), who finds the Jacob–Esau episode to have reached its final shape in a postexilic milieu. Although his arguments are weak, his results are still of interest.

4. Cf. Fokkelman, *Narrative Art in Genesis*, p. 2.

5. Fokkelman himself (*Narrative Art in Genesis*, p. 3) endorses such an order. The 'recreation' (reading, interpretation) of a text should, in his view, precede its 'creation' (studying its growth).

The Forsaken First-Born

Gunkel and Eissfeldt on the Growth of the Jacob–Esau Complex
O. Eissfeldt and H. Gunkel represent distinctly divergent lines of
study on the Jacob–Esau story, and the opinions of other scholars can
often be related or even retraced to their approaches.[1]
In Gunkel's view, the Jacob story should be divided into four groups
of sagas, one of which is the Jacob–Esau complex, and the others the
Jacob–Laban stories, cult sagas connected with cultic sites instituted by
Jacob, and stories about Jacob's children.[2] These constituent elements
were melted together into a fairly well-arranged whole ('zu einer
verhältnismässig guten Einheit verwoben'). The process involved
fusing together the Jacob–Esau and the Jacob–Laban complexes, with
the former providing the frame into which the latter was incorporated. This incorporation was not a loose redactional process but a
careful artistic composition.[3] Even before this, Gunkel has traced the
formation of the Jacob–Esau complex to a development in two
separate stages:

1. A non-Israelite stage in which 'Jacob' and 'Esau' did not
   stand for nations, but 'types' or social classes (perhaps even
   deities originally). They typified the shepherd and the hunts-
   man.[4] Gunkel's well-known designation for these stories is
   Standes-märchen. Their significance lay in the contrast of the
   two types ('brothers') to illustrate their struggle for primacy.[5]
2. In the second stage, the significance of these earlier 'typlogies'
   was nationalized, so that the contesting heroes became Israel
   and Edom. The social sagas were historicized into national
   sagas and became *Völkersagen*. But the identification with
   Israel–Edom fitted the real history of Israel and Edom very
   poorly. The Jacob of the saga is a mild character, not out-
   standingly brave or warlike, whereas in history it was Israel

1.   Cf. also the names mentioned by C. Westermann, *Genesis 12–36*, pp. 495-
96.
2.   Gunkel, *Genesis*, p. 291.
3.   Gunkel, *Genesis*, pp. 292-93.
4.   Cf. Gunkel, *Genesis*, pp. xviii, 316. Similarly M. Noth, *Überlieferungsgeschichte des Pentateuch* (Stuttgart: Kohlhammer, 1948), pp. 105-107, who linked
the stories to small-cattle breeders in Transjordan.
5.   Cf. Gunkel *Genesis*, p. 316. Eising (*Formgeschichtliche Untersuchung zur
Jakobserzählung der Genesis*, pp. 32-35) raises some points of criticism against
Gunkel.

rather than Edom that was the victorious power. In the saga, Esau's main characteristic is his stupidity, but in reality Edom was renowned for wisdom (e.g. Jer. 49.7; Job 2.11). In short, it is 'totally unclear' what prompted scholars to conclude that the existing peoples of Israel and Edom were intended.[1] The second stage also gave a different meaning to the whole complex, which Gunkel describes by the word 'Segen'. In the 'blessing' the specifically Israelite element of the story expressed itself.

When it comes to literary sources, Gunkel thought that the fusion between various elements in the Jacob Cycle could have taken place before J/E set to work, although it is no longer possible to decide whether the fusion happened at the oral or written level.[2] The impetus behind Gunkel's work was to find a situation matching the various conflicting motifs in the stories. Identifying the disparate layers of tradition would tell more about their origin and background than simply differentiating between sources.[3]

One of Gunkel's achievements was his recognition of the clear difference in atmosphere and general milieu between Genesis 25 and 27 and Genesis 32–33. The motifs of 'prediction' and 'fulfilment' are realized very differently in each case. In 25.23, the 'prediction' (clearly a *vaticinium ex eventu*), concerning Jacob is that he will be served by his elder brother, and 27.29 reiterates this:

> Let peoples serve you,
> and nations bow down to you.
> Be lord over your brothers,
> and may your mother's sons bow
> down to you (compare also 27.40).

In chs. 32–33, however, a very different picture emerges as Jacob meets Esau after their long separation. Jacob repeatedly calls himself 'servant' in front of Esau, who accordingly is addressed as Jacob's 'lord'. Jacob prostrates himself before Esau seven times, as does all his household (33.3, 6, 7). Of course, Jacob's behaviour is in accordance

---

1. Cf. Gunkel, *Genesis*, p. 316.
2. Cf. Gunkel, *Genesis*, pp. 292-94, also xix.
3. But on the plural 'brothers' in 27.29, 37, cf. above on 16.12. Gunkel's point that there are 'many brothers' in the blessing and only two in the stories does not give the whole truth.

with the etiquette prescribed for that situation, but it is noteworthy that when Esau addresses Jacob, he simply calls him 'my brother' (33.9).[1] This difference, though of interest from a literary point of view, receives little attention from Fishbane or Fokkelman, nor, for that matter, from Westermann or von Rad.[2] Only Bar-Efrat (referring also to 2 Sam. 13.11) makes a comment to the effect that polite speech reflects feelings of guilt on the part of the speaker, and also a desire to appease the brother.[3] Naturally there are other contrasts, and these will be accounted for later.

Of course, contrasts between the various elements in a story can demonstrate the literary skill of the narrator; but the differing modes of speech in 32–33 and 25–27 should also be understood as a commentary on the Jacob–Esau story as a whole. The open conflict was a theological problem that was only solved by supplementing the story with this resolution. O. Eissfeldt (whose understanding of the patriarchal narratives is said by Thompson to have achieved the status of 'received opinion' among many modern scholars)[4] displays a much stronger interest in questions of sources, since he wants to determine the background of the Jacob Cycle (and the Pentateuchal material in general). As a result, he concentrates on the question of how the Pentateuchal material should be apportioned between the written sources. He draws the following picture:[5]

25.19-20	P
21-26a	L
27-28	J or E
29-34	L

---

1. On this, cf. also Westermann, *Genesis 12–36*, p. 639; von Rad, *Genesis*, p. 266.

2. Westermann (*Genesis 12–36*, p. 617) perceives in 32.4-5 a clear instance of the commissioning formula for a messenger (*Botensendung*). What takes place in 33.1-7 would also be perfectly appropriate for a vassal before his overlord; cf. p. 639. Similarly von Rad, *Genesis*, pp. 257, 266; Skinner, *Genesis*, p. 413. They all refer to or quote the formula of homage in the Tel El Amarna-Tablets: 'At the feet of my Lord, my Sun, I fall down seven and seven times'.

3. Cf. Bar-Efrat, *Narrative Art*, p. 67.

4. Cf. Thompson, 'Conflict Themes in the Jacob Narratives', p. 8.

5. O. Eissfeldt, *Einleitung in das Alte Testament: Unter Einschluss der Apokryphen und Pseudepigraphen. . .Entstehungsgeschichte des Alten Testaments* (Neue Theologische Grundrisse; Tübingen: Mohr, 2nd edn, 1956), pp. 224, 231, 237-38.

26.34-35	P
27	J or E
32.1-24a	J or E
33.1-16	J or E

It is clear from this that what Gunkel saw as the original Jacob–Esau (pre-J/E) 'type' sagas, Eissfeldt assigns to his 'laysource', 'L'. However, for practical purposes, the views of Eissfeldt and Gunkel can easily be reconciled, since in Eissfeldt's understanding the 'L' source is the oldest (it dates back to a period between 950–850 BC) and most 'primitive' among the Pentateuchal sources.

The L source represents the early humans as nomads (against the agriculturalists of J and E), and from a formal point of view its main characteristic is the single, unconnected story-unit.[1] This characteristic is evident in the Jacob–Esau stories. In L's version the individual stories appear in marked isolation. After Esau has lost his birthright, he leaves for Edom, disappears, and never meets Jacob again (25.29-34). There is, in other words, no question of a reunion in 'L'. Jacob's reunion is not with Esau but with *El* (32.24-33). It is only through the work of J and E that the Jacob–Laban story has been absorbed into the Jacob–Esau complex. Here, Eissfeldt and Gunkel agree. However, unlike Gunkel, who sees the national element as the distinctive criterion for deciding between older and later material, Eissfeldt understands Esau's loss of his birthright to imply that Esau relinquishes all claims to the land of Canaan. For Eissfeldt, Gen. 25.21-26 illustrates one particular kind of saga, the *Stammes- und Volkessage*, whose principal interest is the collective (the tribe, the people) in contrast to a genre that focuses on the individual, such as Genesis 27. Consequently, both types are old, although the second type demonstrates a more developed form of saga, the aim of which was the establishment of family links between individuals such as those between the individual Patriarchs.[2] On this point Gunkel and Eissfeldt are opposed. Oddly enough, that does not, as we have seen, affect their view of which texts should be regarded as older.

---

1. Cf. Eissfeldt, *Einleitung*, pp. 230-36.
2. Cf. Eissfeldt, *Einleitung*, p. 233, also p. 44. It seems that the two elements, the collective and the individual, are conflated in Gen. 27 if those two passages in Eissfeldt are combined.

The Texts

The book of Genesis contains a wide variety of texts involving Esau—
conspicuously wider, in fact, than those about Ishmael. They may be
systematically arranged covering his life as follows:

Birth	25.21-26
Adolescence and occupation	25.27
Loss of birthright	25.29-34
Wives	26.34;
Marries Ishmael's daughter	28.6-9; cf. also 36.2-3
Loss of Isaac's blessing	27.1-40
Lives in Seir	32.3
Reunion with Jacob	33.1-15
Parts company with Jacob	33.16; 36.6-7
Returns to Seir	33.16; 36.8
Buries his father	35.29
Genealogy	36.9-18

We are also told of other things between these major events, such as
Esau's plans to murder Jacob (27.41).

As can be seen from the above arrangment, the texts do not form
any unified and consistent portrayal of Esau, and the information
given is partly contradictory or otherwise in tension.

Genesis 25.19-34

Structure and Content. A brief summary of characters in the condensed style of P forms the prologue to the new section in Genesis 25
and to the whole Jacob Cycle. The narrative proper commences in
v. 21, and the subsequent verses will be taken in portions, as follows:

A	21-23	The Birth of Esau and Jacob is prepared
B	24-28	Their birth and growth
C	29-34	Esau loses his birthright

The passage as a whole gives an impression of considerable instability.
Five of the eight verses preceding C introduce a new section or sub-
section by the use of a full verbal sentence (main verb and subject).
Thus, each verse expresses a single thought and the events rapidly suc-
ceed each other. This underlines the introductory character of the
passage.

(20	Isaac is forty years old)
21	Isaac prays—Yahweh consents to remove Rebecca's barrenness—Rebecca conceives
22a-b	The children (habbānîm) struggle within her—'why is it that way with me?'
22c-23	(a subordinate section) She went to inquire of Yahweh—Yahweh answered
24	'Her days were fulfilled for her to be delivered'—twins in her womb
25-26	The first came forth—afterwards his brother came forth
27	(Isaac 60 years old) The boys (hanneʿārîm) grew up
28	Isaac loved—Rebecca loved

Although there may be some kind of leading idea or theme here (such as the concentric structure suggested by Fokkelman for vv. 20-26),[1] this passage does not call for any particular structural organization (as Fokkelman himself is aware). The one idea that is clearly prefigured in the passage is the lurking conflict between Jacob and Esau. It is presented as an irrevocable fact at the start of their lives. Furthermore, its irrevocable nature is even ratified by Yahweh's oracle. The conflict theme is strongly underscored by the effective use of a number of terms indicating kinship and other forms of belonging:[2] 'the children within her', 'twins', 'brother', and 'the boys grew up (together)'. Against these are set up their opposing terms, expressions of conflict: 'struggled with each other'.

Verse 23. At the centre of this section is the oracle sought for and received by Rebecca.[3] It takes the common bilinear form in which each line consists of a double hemistich:

(a) *šʿnê gōyîm bᵉbiṭnēk ûšᵉnê lᵉ' ummîm mimmēʿayik yippārēdû*

(b) *ûlᵉ' ōm mil'ōm yeʿᵉmāṣ wᵉrab yaʿᵃbōd ṣāʿîr*

yippārēdû—'they shall be divided'—forms a fourth element in (a),[4] which once again draws attention to the idea of necessary separation. However closely they are bound together in their mother's womb and

1. Cf. Fokkelman, *Narrative Art in Genesis*, p. 93.
2. An effect not mentioned by Fokkelman or Fishbane.
3. Cf. Fokkelman, *Narrative Art in Genesis*, p. 93.
4. Cf. Fokkelman, *Narrative Art in Genesis*, p. 89.

at birth (Jacob holding fast to Esau's heel, v. 26!), separation is still the predestined lot.

The oracle is a poetic piece interrupting the routine report of Jacob's and Esau's infancy.[1] It is probably intended to imitate a birth oracle, although compared with Gen. 16.11-12 the form has been greatly modified. The introduction to the oracle does conform to the genre: 'She went to inquire of Yahweh, and Yahweh answered her'. The first line, 'Two nations in your womb, two peoples from inside you shall split up', would then correspond to Gen. 16.11 in the sense that it predicts a birth ('in your *womb*', 'from your *inside*'), while the following stich, 'The one shall be stronger than the other; the older shall serve the younger', contains the *vaticinium ex eventu*. In fact, the oracle not only announces the birth of twin sons but foretells the history of two entire peoples. There is a discrepancy between 25.23 and its immediate context—as there is between 16.12 and 27.29 and their particular contexts. The surrounding story concerns individuals, whereas v. 23 has a collective significance and concerns two nations. There are two possible solutions to this problem: 1. The oracle represents a piece of inherited tradition, originally independent of the context; or 2. it is a later composition, created exclusively for its present setting. B.O. Long opts for solution 1. In his opinion, vv. 22-23 'were originally independent and joined, probably at the literary stage in the history of tradition, to the report of the birth of Esau and Jacob'. He believes that Gen. 21.24-26b existed as a separate literary unit, in roughly their present form, and originated from oral tradition. The verses belong together on the grounds that the narrative motifs of barren wife and birth (together with naming) frequently appear together.[2] His position fails to account for the following questions: (a) what was the original setting of the verses; and (b) when were they joined to their present context?

---

1. The break between the poem and its setting (see above) is passed over by Fokkelman, in my view rather casually, as he sums up his treatment: 'This is not the story of just any twins but about children whose whole lives are going to pass under a very special sign, whose destiny and mutual relationship were decisively determined and predicted by Providence before their birth' (*Narrative Art in Genesis*, p. 94). Fokkelman fails to recognize the essential and original distinction between the context of the story and that of the poem.

2. B.O. Long, *The Problem of Etiological Narrative in the Old Testament* (BZAW, 108; Berlin: de Gruyter, 1968), p. 50.

The first question invites many possible answers. If 25.23 is considered independently from its present setting there is ample evidence of conflicts in Israel's history between adversaries that might be thought of symbolically in terms such as 'younger'/'older' or 'victorious'/'submitting'. Within the Israelite nation itself there are the notorious conflicts between distinguished individuals like Saul and David, although they could hardly be described as 'brothers' in any narrow sense. Or, on a national level, the conflict could reflect the political tension between North and South in Israel. But although Judah and Israel are in fact designated (in Edom's mouth!) as 'two nations' (*gōyîm*) and 'two countries' (*'^arāṣôt*) in Ezek. 35.10, the vision of Israel's fundamental unity remained alive in the national consciousness, as witnessed by the prophets. Best of all, the poem probably referred from the beginning to a foreign tribe, and, in the light of its history from the time of David (under whom it was subjugated, 2 Sam. 8.14), this was most likely Edom. This long period of Israelite rule over Edom lasted until the time of Joram (2 Kgs 8.20-22). As a result, I would favour the second option given above: that the poem is an *ad hoc* composition. The *terminus a quo* for its formation must have been the identification of Esau with Edom (v. 30; also 36.43 etc.). An exact date for this identification is difficult to determine, but it is reasonable to assume that it cannot have antedated David's conquest of Edom.[1] This is clear from the fact that the poem is set into the context of Jacob's and Esau's birth, while at the same time referring to them as two 'nations'. It imitates the tribal oracle in that it preserves the perspective of an individual hero embodying in his person the future of his descendants.

The poem, then, could stem from a time somewhat later than

1. So V. Maag, 'Jakob–Esau–Edom', *TZ* 13 (1957), pp. 418-29 (425-26); G. Wallis, 'Die Tradition von den drei Ahnvätern', *ZAW* 81 (1969), pp. 18-40 (21); J.R. Bartlett, 'The Brotherhood of Edom', *JSOT* 4 (1977), pp. 2-27 (21) (but 'well established no earlier than by the time of the Edomite revolt from Judah'); and, on different grounds, *'āḥ* = 'treaty partner', 'vassal' (following Akkadian): M. Fishbane, 'The Treaty Background of Amos 1:11 and Related Matters', *JBL* 89 (1970), pp. 313-18 (315-17). Blank ('Studies in Post-Exilic Universalism', pp. 176-77, 182-83, 190) dissents from this view, and holds the equation of Esau with Edom to be postexilic. His conclusion rests on a number of suppositions that do not support his own particular construction either. For a historical review of the period of King David, cf. also J.R. Bartlett, *Edom and the Edomites* (JSOTSup, 77; Sheffield: JSOT Press, 1989), pp. 130-33.

David's conquest.[1] The idea of Edom's brotherhood is very much alive in the mind of the Deuteronomist. The fact that Edom is 'your brother' in Deut. 23.8(7) is an imperative for treating him like a fellow Israelite, and for letting him into the Assembly of the Lord[2] (with a proviso that three generations should pass before the stipulation would take effect). Here, however, the name does not carry cultic-ethical implications but is intended to instil a sense of national pride in David's victories. It testifies to the attitude prevailing during the heyday of the Israelite Empire: the younger has overcome the older.

The poem makes two points: that the two nations have a common origin, and that one is stronger ($'m\!ṣ$) than the other. Their relationship is that of lord and servant—compare 2 Sam. 8.14: 'all the Edomites became David's servants'. In Bartlett's opinion,[3] the poem may have been written at any time during Edom's long period of subservience to Judah, or even after it. I would not allow for such a long timespan, since the poem is filled with a conquering spirit inconceivable a long time after the event itself.[4]

Verses 24-28. With Gen. 25.24-28 the narrative resumes its focus on individuals, the twins to be born. Verse 24 forms the logical continuation not of 22, but of 21. As these verses now stand, the word 'children' in v. 22 requires the information given in v. 24, since it is not until that verse that we are informed that Rebecca was pregnant not with one child but with twins.

Again, there is a contrast implied here in the word 'twins' ($t'wmym$). Traditionally, it would have been expected for twin brothers to be alike in appearance and character (as are Simeon and Levi in Gen. 49.5). Here, however, the narrator surprises the reader: the two babies are

1. Westermann (*Genesis 12–36*, pp. 503-505) places it in the early days of the (united) monarchy.
2. Cf. Bartlett, 'The Brotherhood of Edom', pp. 5-6. He is not quite satisfied with von Rad's cultic explanation; cf. above.
3. Cf. Bartlett, 'The Brotherhood of Edom', p. 19.
4. For a different opinion on this, see Thompson, 'Conflict Themes in the Jacob Narratives', p. 16: 'the past "ancestral event" is not oriented by the narrator to either his contemporary world or to the world of the historical past of Israel and Edom'. Thompson's assertion is that the poem claims 'superiority-by-association' on the part of the Israelite narrator. That assertion does not, however, annul an explanation in historical terms, since a claim of superiority reveals a psychological attitude which is very likely to have been nurtured by contemporary events.

of starkly different looks. Esau is 'red' (*'dmwny*), 'like a hairy garment' (*k' drt s'r*). The epithets given to each of them are clearly also intended as etymologies. Esau is named after his looks, whereas Jacob, in contrast, is named after an action of his: 'his hand grasping Esau's heel' (*b'qb 'sw*).

In fact, only for Jacob is the etymology compatible with the name. As has been pointed out by Westermann and others,[1] two etymological explanations are given for Esau, but neither actually produces the name 'Esau'. It is 'Edom' and 'Seir' that seem to have been in the author's mind. Seir was the home of Esau according to Gen. 36.8 (compare also Deut. 2.4; Josh. 24.2-4) and in the Song of Deborah (Judg. 5.4). Edom and Seir are regarded as parallels, as in Num. 24.18. The mention of the two names together indicates a close connection (if not identification) between them, and it is likely that Esau was originally connected with Seir and only subsequently with Edom as the 'motherland' of Seir.[2] The word *'dmwny* may then have been an addition intended to establish Esau's connection with Edom.[3] (If it was an addition, it could of course have been much later than the identification itself.) In any case it is clear that the equation of Esau with Seir-Edom lies behind the present text. What the etymology explains is not the proper name itself, but the nature of Esau's connection with his land. He is, so to speak, the embodiment of Seir-Edom.

A colour also features in the parallel story of 38.27-30 (a variant story according to Gunkel),[4] in which Esau's second name, like that of Jacob (*peres* from *pārastā*), is explained (v. 29). In each case, the etymology seems forced and awkward. In the case of Zerah, a 'scarlet thread' is bound to the hand of the first twin to appear; and again, the

1. Westermann, *Genesis 12–36*, p. 505. Cf. Maag, 'Jakob–Esau–Edom', p. 422. G. Wallis ('Die Tradition von den drei Ahnvätern', p. 20: 'behaart' for *'ēsāw*) is not correct; no such adjective is found in the text.
2. Cf. J.R. Bartlett, 'The Land of Seir and the Brotherhood of Edom', *JTS* NS 20 (1969), pp. 1-20 (10). The fact that he renounces the thesis of the earlier article in 'The Brotherhood of Edom' (p. 26 n. 68) does not affect an understanding of Esau–Seir as originally separate from Edom. Cf. also L.E. Axelsson, *The Lord Rose up from Seir: Studies in the History and Traditions of the Negev and Southern Judah* (ConBOT, 23; Lund: Gleerup, 1987), p. 70.
3. Cf. Bartlett, 'The Land of Seir', p. 11; Blank, 'Studies in Post-Exilic Universalism', p. 177. On the other hand, Westermann (*Genesis 12–36*, p. 505) suggests that both 'red' and 'hairy' functioned here like *'admônî* describing the handsomeness of David in 1 Sam. 16.12; 17.42.
4. Cf. Gunkel, *Genesis*, pp. 418-19.

colour only indirectly alludes to the name (*zerah* = 'sunrise'). Apparently the common letters *š* and *n* in *šānî* and *ri' šōnâ* provoked the comment 'this one appeared first' (although 'second' would have been just as appropriate in view of Hebrew *šny*). Only later would the name Zerah have been associated with the colour *šny*. Both versions show a common tendency. Jacob's name was traced to an action on his part, whereas Esau's was explained by association with the coulour 'red' or 'crimson'. A clear connection between the etymology and the name of the second brother need never have existed (although it is possible that another, more appropriate adjective was replaced by *'dmwny*).

Unlike vv. 29-34, the latter passage does not form a continuous narrative. Instead, it is a statement of certain facts that introduce the Jacob–Esau complex. In its present shape, the passage seems to bear the marks of P (e.g. data about age), although, as indicated above, much earlier material must have been incorporated. Westermann's suggestion that a redactor was responsible for the combination of P and J material for 26b may well be correct.[1]

Verses 29-34. Gen. 25.29 begins a new narrative section with a proper plot, and the passage is best subjected to a structural analysis such as Fokkelman's, rather than to a redactional analysis as in the former section.

Esau and Jacob are the sole characters in this drama.[2] Their roles are brought into focus by the overture and finale of the story. The drama begins with Jacob boiling a stew and ends in Esau renouncing his birthright. In this case Fokkelman's arrangement and analysis of the verses in chiastic order is convincingly clear (even though questions may be raised as to the formal nature of this chiasm). I reproduce it here in a shortened form.[3]

> A (29a)   Jacob is boiling pottage
>   B (29b)   Esau enters, coming from the field
>   C–D–X–D^1 (30-33a) Dialogue
>   C^1 (33b) Jacob gives food and drink to Esau
>   B^1 (34bc)   Esau leaves the scene
> A^1 (34d)   Esau despises his birthright

---

1. Cf. Gunkel, *Genesis*, p. 506.
2. On the story as drama, cf. also Eising, *Formgeschichtliche Untersuchung zur Jakobserzählung*, pp. 21-2, 38-40, 446.
3. Cf. Fokkelman, *Narrative Art in Genesis*, p. 95.

The story may also be examined in terms of the interplay between the two protagonists as it is reflected in the various predicates and verbs.

Verse	Jacob	Esau
29a	was boiling stew	
29b		came in
30		was tired
		said. 'let me gulp!'
		'I am tired'
31	said, '*sell* me'	
32		'I am going to die'
33	said, '*swear* to me!'	
		swore to him
		and *sold* to Jacob
34	*gave* to Esau	
		ate
		drank
		rose
		went
		(comment: despised)

Esau is the subject in 12 cases (including nominal clauses), as against only 4 for Jacob. There is, however, an essential difference in the individual predicates/verbs associated with the respective brothers. Throughout the episode, Jacob is the one who takes the intitiative and determines Esau's behaviour by preparing the food that whets Esau's appetite. This is especially clear from the dialogue.

> 31 Jacob said, 'sell me!'
> 33 Jacob said, 'swear to me!'
> ——and he (Esau) swore to him
> and he sold to Jacob

The plot unfolds in four main stages. In each stage Esau's conduct follows as a reaction to an initiative of Jacob's. The only important transitive verb of which Esau is the subject is 'sold', and this only heightens Esau's ordeal; he has no other choice but to sell the one single asset of which he is in full possession, his birthright. This is given in exchange for his life ('I am about to die'). Although he is a hunter, he is unable to provide meat for himself but is dependent on Jacob's offer of 'bread and pottage of lentils' (25.34), products of the soil.

Most of the other verbs associated with Esau are intransitive verbs of motion: 'came in (and was tired)', 'rose', 'went', and so on.[1] Through this imbalance in the number of verbs for Esau, the narrator clearly suggests that Esau will be the loser from the outset.[2] This is accentuated by the concluding remark: 'Esau despised his birthright'. 'Despised' sums up the sequence and evaluates Esau's action morally (on the basis of Esau's belittling remark in v. 32). 'Despise' also signifies Esau's attitude judged from the point of view of the redactor, who at this point also represents the reader in being the 'spectator' of the dramatic 'performance'.

The central noun in the story is *bkrh*, 'birthright'. It appears as the object of the important verb 'sell' in vv. 31 and 33, and of the moral evaluation in v. 34. It is also the object of 'despised' in v. 32. The only thing Esau really owns is not good enough for him because it cannot be eaten!

Excursus: The Birthright in the Milieu of the Old Testament

The contest between the brothers in ch. 25 was about the right of primogeniture, *bᵉkôrâ*. The origin of this term lies probably in ancient agricultural rites in which the first-fruit and the first-born were sacrificed to the gods. A version of this practice is prescribed by Num. 3.40-43, where Moses is commanded to count the first-born males and then to redeem them by consecrating the Levites to Yahweh as his special property. The reason for the command is given in 3.12-13: the slaying of the Egyptian first-born during Passover.

> Behold, I have taken the Levites from among the people of Israel instead of every first-born that opens the womb among the people of Israel. The Levites shall be mine, for all the first-born are mine; on the day that I slew all the first-born in the land of Egypt, I consecrated for my own all the first-born in Israel, both of man and of beast; they shall be mine, I am the Lord.

Although the birth of the first-born son primarily laid a cultic obligation on the father, it could also be seen as proof of the father's procreative power. The first-born could thus be spoken of in poetic terms as his father's 'strength' and his 'first-fruit', or 'the firstling of vigour'—Gen. 49.3; Deut. 21.17; Pss. 78.51; 105.30. (In Deut. 33.17 a

---

1.   O. Eissfeldt ('Stammessage und Novelle in den Geschichten von Jakob und von seinen Söhnen', in *idem*, *Kleine Schriften*, I [ed. R. Sellheim and F. Mass; Tübingen: Mohr, 1962], pp. 84-104 [93]) interprets 'rose and went' as Esau leaving his country and settling in Seir, which would mean reading the whole context of the Jacob–Esau complex into this single episode.

2.   Berlin (*Poetics and Interpretation*, p. 39) takes Esau's speech and action to be markers of his 'primitive' character, both repulsive and eliciting pity; cf. also p. 120, and Sternberg, *Poetics*, p. 157.

link is made with the animal kingdom. The first-born is compared to the first-born ox.) A first-born daughter ($b^ek\hat{\imath}r\hat{a}$) is mentioned in Gen. 19.31.

The rules adhering to the rights of the first-born created a well-defined hierarchy among the male offspring within a family. The first-born was entitled to certain rights of inheritance. According to Deut. 21.17 his father had to grant him a greater share than the other sons (*py šnym*), often interpreted as 'two thirds', but better still 'a double share'—twice the remaining brothers' individual shares[1] (cf. 2 Kgs 2.9). The basis for measuring out the share was 'everything that [the father] possessed', in other words, the whole estate. However, the Deuteronomic passage as a whole (21.15-17) is concerned with the problem of who should be the lawful first-born in cases where the father has had sons by two wives. The legislation seems to pertain to a specific case, even if 'the right of the first-born' (*mišpaṭ habb^ekōrâ*) probably had a more general application. Tsevat believes that this 'right' to inherit more than an equal portion was no more than an expression of a widespread appreciation of the eldest son above the other children.[2]

The preferential position of the eldest son was not unique to Israel in the ancient Near East. There are, for example, Akkadian terms which, although etymologically different, can be directly compared with the Old Testament. One is *maru rabu*, 'eldest son' (cf. Gen. 27.42: *habbēn haggādōl*).[3] Another is *aplu*, 'heir, oldest son (one enjoying a preferential status), son'.[4] Although the Code of Hammurabi does not contain any reference to the privileged status of the eldest son as a set rule, it lays down at least one case when the first-born is entitled to a preferential share of father's property. Paragraph 170 reads:

> If a freeman's wife bore him children, and his female slave bore him children too, and the father in his lifetime said to the children whom the female slave had born him: 'My children', counting them together with the children of the wife; then, after the father has

---

1.   So M. Tsevat, 'בְּכֹר', *ThWAT*, I, cols. 643-50 (648). On the basis of an Akkadian text, H. Donner ('Adoption oder Erwägungen zur Adoption im Alten Testament auf dem Hintergrund der altorientalischen Rechte', *Or Ant* [1969], pp. 87-119 [95 n.]) gives the formula: 'E:B ×2' for the first-born's portion, where E = the property, B = number of sons.

2.   Cf. Tsevat, 'בְּכֹר', col. 648; also cols. 645-46 for corresponding terms in Ancient Mesopotamia.

3.   Cf. Tsevat, 'בְּכֹר', cols. 645-46.

4.   Cf. *CAD*, I/2, pp. 173-77. The texts quoted there mostly contain declarations about who should be the rightful heir. Cf. also W. von Soden (ed.), *Akkadisches Handwörterbuch unter Benutzung des lexikalischen Nachlasses von Bruno Meissner (1868-1947)*. I. *A–L* (Wiesbaden: Otto Harrassowitz, 1965), p. 58; R. Borger, *Babylonisch-assyrische Lesestücke*. I. *Die Texte in Umschrift*. II. *Elemente der Grammatik und der Schrift. Glossar. Die Texte in Keilschrift* (AnOr, 54; Rome: Pontificium Institutum Biblicum, 2nd edn, 1979), p. 240.

died, the sons of the wife and the sons of the female slave share equally in the property of the father's house; the first-born [*aplum*], the son of the wife chooses and takes a(n additional) share.[1]

Here, the first-born is explicitly granted a preferential status, although this may apply only to the case in question.[2] Paragraph 165 states that the father may bequeath his first-born, 'who is his favourite' (literally 'the first one in his eye') a special gift, and the first-born then has the right to take possession of that extra portion. Otherwise, he has to share equally with the others.

The lawcode of Lipit-Ishtar (19th cent. BC) ruled (par. 24) that the children of a first wife must divide equally with those of a second. Paragraph 32 reckons with the possibility that the father can set aside a bethrothal gift for his eldest son ('the big brother') while he is still alive, but due to a long lacuna in the text it is not possible to define the context any further.[3]

From the area of private law, two further documents dealt with by Mendelsohn deserve attention. One is an adoption contract from Mari, from the time of the Assyrian domination.[4] The contract prescribes two shares for the first-adopted son in case more sons should be adopted; the younger sons then divide the remaining inheritance in equal shares between themselves. Similar regulations concerning the first-born (not adopted) son are known from Nippur, so that Mendelsohn concludes that before Hammurabi, not only in Assyria and Nuzi, but also in Babylonia (Southern and Northern) the first-born was treated to a 'double share' or an 'additional share' in the paternal estate. He concludes from Deut. 21.15-17 that the same custom was also prevalent in Palestine (compare Joseph's *šᵉkem 'aḥad 'al-'aḥêkā*, Gen. 48.22).

The second document is a marriage contract between one Irihalpa and the woman Naidu from among the Alalakh tablets (15th cent.), published by D.J. Wiseman in 1953.[5]

1.   For the Akkadian text, see Borger, *Babylonisch-assyrische Lesestücke*, II, p. 301 (transcription in I, p. 33). I. Mendelsohn ('On the Preferential Status of the Eldest Son', *BASOR* 156 [1959], pp. 38-40 [40 n.]) interprets *aplum* in a collective sense, and so understands the paragraph to imply that the sons of a freeborn wife and those born by a slave-concubine whom the father had adopted shall divide equally; but the sons of the freeborn wife shall choose their shares first, which means that they are able to reserve the best part of the estate for themselves. I take the singular *aplum mar hirtim* to be a real singular.

2.   Cf. Tsevat, 'בְּכֹר', col. 646, who does not mention this individual case, although he refers to par. 170.

3.   For a suggested context, see Kramer's translation in *ANET*, pp. 159-61.

4.   Cf. Mendelsohn, 'On the Preferential Status', p. 38. The same text is also dealt with by Donner, 'Adoption oder Legitimation?', pp. 95-96, 116.

5.   D.J. Wiseman (ed.), *The Alalakh Tablets* (London: British Institute of Archeology at Ankara, 1953), §92.

If Naidu does not give birth to a son, [then] the daughter of his brother Iwashshura shall be given [to Irihalpa as a wife]; if [another wife] of Irihalpa gives birth to a son first, and after that Naidu gives birth to a son, the son of Naidu alone shall be the first-born.[1]

The special status as first-born could in this case be transferred from one son to another.

In the light of ancient Near Eastern custom, it is clear that the first-born status must have been an attractive one, and the marriage contract demonstrates that a father could decide to which of his sons he would give it. In this way the laws of primogeniture could be 'disregarded' (Mendelsohn), or at least suspended.

How is this material relevant to the Old Testament?[2] Although the Alalakh document does not state whether the second wife was a slave, the possibility cannot be excluded; if so, it would be a parallel case for that of Isaac and Ishmael. Gen. 21.10 makes it clear that it is the threat of Ishmael sharing in Abraham's inheritance that provokes Sarah's action against him. According to the Alalakh contract, Ishmael could be ousted from his position as first-born, but would still probably be entitled to a share in the property. Deut. 21.15-17 was intended to prevent this kind of arbitrariness in the granting of first-born status, and to institute uniform legal practice.[3]

More generally, I would conclude that the concepts and customs connected with the first-born status were commonplace in the world of the Old Testament and hence needed no further explication or definition. As noted above, Deut. 21.15-17 does not, strictly speaking, give any 'code' of birthright, but merely abrogates an earlier practice. This applies to private civil law; in questions pertaining to the cultic laws such as firstlings and first-fruits, the Old Testament is more outspoken.

Whatever the origin of the story in Gen. 25.29-34,[4] it is certainly very ancient. Gunkel assigns it to the E source.[5] It is clear that in the original story Esau and Jacob were not regarded as representatives of nations. The comment in 30b, 'Therefore he was called Edom', is a later parenthetical remark. (Fokkelman too, even though he later contends that 'there is not a word too many' in the story, disposes of it as the narrator's 'nod to his listeners' and not part of the plot itself.[6]) It is evidently a response to *hāʾādōm*, which must then have belonged to the original story; and if it was original here, so it must have been

1. The text is quoted from Mendelsohn, 'On the Preferential Status', p. 38.
2. Sternberg (*Poetics*, p. 183) questions its relevance, against A. Speiser.
3. Cf. von Rad, *Deuteronomium*, pp. 98-99.
4. Westermann, *Genesis 12–36*, p. 508; Maag ('Jakob–Esau–Edom', p. 424) calls it a 'cultural myth'.
5. Cf. Gunkel, *Genesis*, p. 297; Eissfeldt (*Einleitung*, p. 88) calls it the 'tribal saga' of the L-source.
6. Cf. Fokkelman, *Narrative Art in Genesis*, p. 95 n. 13; Maag, 'Jakob–Esau–Edom', p. 423.

in v. 25. Westermann proposes that the original beginning of the story
has been lost, as it now starts rather abruptly in v. 29.[1] However, I do
not see that it is necessary, and Westermann himself does not state any
argument in defence of this. Nor do I see any reason to regard the
present introduction as redactional—it states just as much as is needed
to understand the further development of the plot. On the other hand,
the closing words, 'so Esau despised. . .', are a redactional comment,
conveying the condensed moral lesson of the story: 'he despised his
birthright'—well, then, he deserves only contempt for himself!

Clearly, the significance of the birthright is essential to the story.
What Esau has at his free disposal at the beginning, Jacob has actively
struggled for and obtained by the end. In my understanding, the word
beḵōrâ is used here with its fullest significance, and concerns the
brothers' access to their rights as both members of a social group,
principally the family, and of distinct occupational classes.

There is an important overlap between these two categories—family
and trade—that tends to be blurred by too rigid a classification of the
story either as 'family saga' or 'cultural myth'. If the cultural element
is seen to be dominant, the result is often a distortion of the whole plot
and an underestimation of the narrator's technique and skill. This is
what happpens in the case of Maag's interpretation, according to
which the 'myth' reflects the transition from a culture of hunters to
one of cattle holders.[2]

Maag's may be a 'demythologized' interpretation, but it is also an
allegorization: the *beḵōrâ* is no more than the hunter's right to his own
hunting grounds.[3] This is a good illustration of how, in biblical
scholarship, Old Testament 'myths' used to be seen as reflections
either of historical and sociological developments in early Israelite
society, or of psychological processes in the 'primitive' human mind.[4]
If treated like this, the story looses its literary cohesion and falls

---

1. Cf. Westermann, *Genesis 12–36*, p. 509.

2. Cf. Maag, 'Jakob–Esau–Edom', p. 424. Westermann (*Genesis 12–36*,
p. 509) points out the value of the story from a cultural historical aspect.

3. Blum (*Vätergeschichte*, p. 481) is critical of such allegorizing approaches in
this context. Before him, Eising (*Formgeschichtliche Untersuchung zur
Jakobserzählung*, p. 43) had pointed out that the issue of land possession cannot
account for all details in the story, e.g. the bias towards an ethical evaluation of the
characters.

4. Cf. Rogerson's systematization of the different meanings of 'myth' in Old
Testament scholarship (*Myth in Old Testament Interpretation*, pp. 174-76).

apart—it is no longer a 'story' but an allegory about the development of various cultural forms in an ancient society.

An interpretation of the patriarchal stories as family stories is strongly advocated by Westermann. This has the benefit of avoiding arbitrary reinterpretations; the story is left intact and taken at its face value. In Westermann's opinion, the story goes back to the patriarchal age and illustrates the conflict raging within a particular family. But Westermann's position does have its weaknesses. Blum questions Westermann's uncritical equation of the patriarchs with real historical figures.[1] For Blum the patriarchal stories are primarily to be understood as etiologies of 'Israel', and not traceable to any pre-Israelite nomadic ('patriarchal') age. They were constructed from the perspective of an Israel already in existence, and their purpose is to explain Israel's antecedents and relations to surrounding peoples. They are certainly concerned with 'history', but they do not reflect history in the way earlier scholars believed. The family perspective was a given; the narrator had no other alternative. Only for the nomadic element in the stories is Blum willing to consider 'some sort of collective memory of Israel's past', but he immediately qualifies this concession and warns against drawing any conclusions about the hypothetical pre-history of *texts*.[2]

I would broadly subscribe to Blum's theory of how the present text relates to a 'patriarchal' age. But more than Blum, I would stress the presence in Israel of early traditions and their impact on the formation of the patriarchal stories. The categories within which to frame the life-stories of patriarchs were given by tradition: 'My father was a wandering Aramean...' I would also be inclined to replace Blum's 'aetiology' with the term 'organization'. Israel as a nation had to organize the world around it; and not only the world of the present, but that of the past as well. The patriarchal stories represent this retrospective organization.

From a hermeneutical viewpoint, a clear tension exists between the passage as 'story' (e.g. family story) and as *Kulturmythus*. Perhaps that tension should be allowed to exist so as to preserve the interpretative

1. Cf. Blum, *Vätergeschichte*, p. 501. Westermann's supposition that the 'extended family' was the home of the 'saga' as the 'simple form' of more developed literature—a theory based primarily on much later literature than the Old Testament—is criticized by Rogerson, *Anthropology*, pp. 75-77.
2. Cf. Blum, *Vätergeschichte*, pp. 504; cf. also pp. 69, 481.

potentials of the story. An interpretation like Fokkelman's favours such a solution, since it prescribes no particular standard for determining the pre-history of the passage. It can be treated in its own right as literature. A parallel could be drawn with the New Testament parables. Understanding them does not necessarily involve finding a definite historical anchorage for the characters. Nobody asks, 'Did the Prodigal Son really exist?' But the patriarchal stories are not parables, and paying respect to their literary value does not make obsolete the task of investigating their origins.

Summary. What picture of Esau is created by ch. 25? He is, above all, the polar opposite of Jacob. As a result, he is marked off as 'alien' on an individual as well as a national (v. 23) level. Regardless of the original connection between the chapter and the two individuals, the national element greatly influenced the general image of them held by later generations. It is already explicitly alluded to in Gen. 27.30, and it provided fuel for later attacks on Esau. These attacks were made upon him primarily as a representative of an alien nation, but they were also combined with a judgment of him as an 'evil' personality.

Genesis 27

Structure and Content. Genesis 27 is one of the longest coherent and uninterrupted passages in the entire Jacob–Esau cycle. It contains the episode of the deception of Isaac by Rebecca and Jacob, which robs Esau of Isaac's blessing. This happens in a series of scenes in which the protagonists are briefly spotlighted in pairs.[1]

A	1-4	Isaac–Esau
B	5-17	Rebecca and Jacob
C	18-29	Jacob and Isaac
D	30-40	Esau–Isaac
E	41	Esau–Jacob
F	42-45	Rebecca–Jacob
(G	46–28.5	Rebecca–Isaac)

The only characters who never confront each other directly are Rebecca and Esau. Esau and Jacob do not speak to each other. Rebecca speaks about, but not to, Esau in B and F, and the 'Hittite women' she

---

1.   Westermann, *Genesis 12–36*, p. 530, and 'Olrik's laws'.

mentions in G are of course Esau's wives (26.34). Logically, G is not part of the story but forms an introduction to 28.1-5.[1] The division above is formal, whereas Westermann divides the passage according to content: 1-29, The Blessing of Jacob (1-17, Preparation; 18-29, Execution); 30-40, the Blessing of Esau; 41-45, Esau's plans to murder Jacob and Rebecca foils the plan.[2]

Fokkelman[3] discovers another chiastic order.

A	1-5	Isaac and Esau, 'son of the *brkh/bkrh*'
B	6-17	Rebecca sends Jacob onto the stage
C	18-29	Jacob appears before Isaac
C_1	30-40	Esau appears before Isaac
B_1	41-45	Rebecca sends Jacob off the stage
A_1	46+28.1-5	Isaac and 'son of the *brkh/bkrh*'

Fokkelman, too, explains the story by means of theatrical terminology. He speaks of it as an act from a play consisting of six scenes.[4]

The Composition and Aim of Chapter 27. The composition of the chapter has caused much discussion. Gunkel proposes that it is a combination of J and E on the basis of a number of variants within the chapter and the fact that in 32.4-22, 33.1-16 and 35.3, 7 both these sources show a knowledge of the story.[5] On the other hand, as Skinner points out, it is difficult to find any positive arguments for a mixture of sources in the chapter. Skinner himself does find occasional traces of E (in his view vv. 33-34 and 35-38 are duplicates).[6] Westermann, too, recognizes in these verses the only real doublet in the chapter. However, he does concede that they may be explained differently, and that other supposed doublets or contradictions are only apparent.[7] Noth assigns the whole chapter to J, although he expresses some doubts.[8] By comparison, von Rad is open to the idea of more than one

1. Von Rad (*Genesis*, p. 222) divides the passage in a similar way (although mistakenly 'Jakob und Esau' in vv. 1-5).
2. Cf. Westermann, *Genesis 12–36*, p. 529.
3. Fokkelman, *Narrative Art in Genesis*, p. 98.
4. Cf. Fokkelman, *Narrative Art in Genesis*, p. 97; cf. also p. 101.
5. Cf. Gunkel, *Genesis*, pp. 305-306.
6. Cf. Skinner, *Genesis*, pp. 368-69. He also refers to Wellhausen.
7. Cf. Westermann, *Genesis 12–36*, p. 531.
8. Cf. Noth, *Überlieferungsgeschichte*, p. 30 n.

source, if only on the ground of the many repetitions.[1]

In the end, it seems difficult in such a text to find any reliable criteria for discriminating between narrator's licence and genuine variants and contradictions without being unreasonably subjective. What is clear is that the story has undergone some redactional work. So, in 27.36, Esau explicitly refers to the loss of his birthright (narrated in ch. 25). Verse 36ab is probably a later addition. The wordplay *bkrty/brkty* clearly presupposes 25.26 and 25.29-34 (in their present form).

As it stands, the story could have many aims. One is evidently to cut the bonds between Esau and his family, even though it is Jacob who has to abandon his father's house and flee. We are probably to understand that Rebecca has broken with Esau even before the narrative commences (compare Sarah and Ishmael), and during the narrative itself, relations between Jacob and Esau also break down. The relations between Esau and Isaac are not affected. It seems that Isaac's blessing affects only Esau's status relative to Jacob, without banning Esau from the family circle.

The genre of 'blessing' is evident in the farewell speech.[2] In Genesis 25, as in Genesis 48–49, the dying father's last words to his sons and grandchildren are understood as a 'blessing'. The cultic function of the blessing is attested in, for example, Num. 6.24-26 and Ps. 67.2, where it serves to dismiss the congregation at the end of the service (cf. Lev. 9.22; 2 Sam. 6.18). Here, however, the blessing is not the determining element, since—like the 'antiblessing' of 27.39-40[3]—it is the narrative parts, in which the blessing is embedded, that dominate the scene. Yet 'blessing' is still at the heart of the story and the coveted 'object' of the competing brothers.

Verses 27-29. The poetic form of Isaac's blessing interrupts the flow of the narrative (in a way similar to other speeches in the mouth of major biblical figures such as Moses and David). The first blessing, delivered to Jacob (Gen. 27.27-29), is couched in general terms using well-known imagery. The passage may be organized as follows.[4]

---

1. Cf. von Rad, *Genesis*, p. 222.
2. Cf. Westermann, *Genesis 12–36*, p. 532, referring to Gen. 24.60.
3. Cf. Fokkelman, *Narrative Art in Genesis*, p. 98.
4. Cf. Westermann, *Genesis 12–36*, pp. 536-37.

A. Two blessings of fertility	1. Behold, the smell of my son is like the smell of a field which Yahweh has blessed.
	2. May God give you of the dew from heaven, and of the fatness of the earth, and plenty of grain and wine.
B. A blessing of overlordship	Let peoples serve you and nations bow down to you. Be lord over your brothers, and may your mother's sons bow down to you.
C. Conclusion: curse and blessing	Cursed be every one who curses you, and blessed be every one who blesses you.

From a traditio-historical point of view the passage is a synthesis of different sayings. Again, Genesis 49 (together with Deut. 33) provides clear comparisons. So, for example, the use of 'my son' by Jacob is also found in Gen. 49.8 (the oracle to Judah—note the change into a 2nd person verb), and, as here, it suggests a particular degree of intimacy between the father and the son so addressed (for Isaac it is still Esau, his favourite). The exchange of words between Abraham and Isaac in Gen. 22.7-8, on their way to the mountain in the land of Moriah, is also comparable:

> And Isaac said to his father Abraham, 'My father!' And he said, 'Here am I, my son'. He said, 'Behold, the fire and the wood; but where is the lamb for a burnt offering?' Abraham said, 'God will provide himself the lamb for a burnt offering, my son.'

As in Gen. 49.8 one might also expect a 2nd person verb in 25.27, but that alteration takes place only in the next verse. 'The smell of a field which Yahweh has blessed' 27.27 is a clever allusion to the preceding context, and also to 25.27, 29-34: Isaac believes he is talking to Esau, 'the man of the field'. At the same time it alludes to the land of Israel as blessed by Yahweh and given to Abraham and his descendants.

'The dew from heaven and the fatness of the earth' in A.2 recalls the blessing of Joseph in Genesis 49 and Deuteronomy 33, except that there the poetic imagery is on a different level. Gen. 27.28 also lacks the quasi-mythological reference to *thwm*, 'the depth', in the second member.

Gen. 49.25	*brkt šmym m'l—brkt thwm rbṣt tḥt*
Deut. 33.13	*(mmgd) šmym mṭl—wmthwm rbṣt tḥt*
Gen. 27.28	*mṭl hšmym—wmšmny h'rṣ*

A distinctive feature of the poetic language in Genesis 49 and
Deuteronomy 33 are the pairs mother/father, sun/moon and mountains/
hills. Gen. 27.28 lacks these and would then seem to represent only
one part of a larger context of blessing. This underlines further the
compound nature of this section. The references stay consistently
within an agricultural setting; again, compare Gen. 49.11-12: 'fatness
and wine', a formulation dictated by ancient tradition, as Westermann
suggests.[1]

B articulates a wish for overlordship more than actual 'blessing'.
Isaac's wish that his son (whom we know to be Jacob) might be
'served' by other peoples takes on a meaning only within a tribal context in which the 'peoples' and 'nations' would be equivalent to 'your
mother's sons'. (For the significance of 'your brothers', see above).
Elsewhere in the Cycle it is Jacob who is the servant: both of Laban
(29.15, 18) and of Esau (e.g. 32.4), and the concept of 'Jacob the
servant' is of essential theological importance in Deutero-Isaiah. Here,
Jacob is the ancestor of not only the twelve tribes as a whole, but of
Judah (cf. Gen. 49.8) and David in particular, and from that perspective, the 'blessing' is a *vaticinium ex eventu*.

C contains a concluding curse and blessing, which has a literal
parallel in Num. 24.9 (compare also Gen. 12.3). The parallel between
Gen. 27.27-29 and Numbers 24 prompts Westermann to suggest a
roughly similar date for their creation.[2] Apart from this, the parallels
given by Westermann are very general and cannot by themselves
underpin suggestions of a common date. It seems safer to assume that
the passage is a late composition of originally separate elements
(which of course, may themselves be ancient).

Verses 30-40. In Gen. 27.30-40 Jacob departs, Esau comes in from his
hunting tour and the dialogue between himself and Isaac follows.
Compared to the dialogue with the fake Esau, this second dialogue is
marked by a chill sense of distance on Isaac's part. Esau strives for
intimacy ('my father') but Isaac harshly turns him down.

31-32   'Let my father arise, and eat of his son's game. . . '
         Isaac: 'Who are you?'
         'I am your son, your first-born, Esau.'

1.   Cf. Westermann, *Genesis 12–36*, p. 537; he also quotes Ugaritic parallels.
2.   Cf. Westermann, *Genesis 12–36*, p. 538.

34-35	'Bless me, even me also, my father!' *Isaac*: 'Your brother. . .has taken away your blessing.'
36-37	'Have you not reserved a blessing for me?' *Isaac*: 'What then can I do for you, my son?'
38	'Bless me, even me also, my father!'

It is ironic that Isaac does not address Esau as 'my son' until v. 37. Having finally realized the terrible mistake, he gives vent to his feelings for his first-born son.[1] But it is too late; words of consolation cannot undo the mistake; there is simply nothing more to be done.

Esau's repeated cry, 'Bless me, even me also, my father!' may be imitating cultic language. Just as the supplication in Ps. 31.17, 'Let Thy face shine on Thy servant' receives the response, 'The Lord make his face shine upon you', so the Priestly blessing 'The Lord bless you . . . ' may have answered the supplication 'Bless me, O Lord' (or 'Have mercy on me, O Lord', 'Save me, my God'; e.g. Pss. 6.3; 9.14; 51.3; 56.2; also cf. 3.8; 54.3). This is all the more likely since here there is a ceremonial air given to the blessing, as shown by the festive clothing in v. 15[2] (although Gen. 27.34 and 38 are the only occurrences of the *piel* imperf. of *brk* with 1st person singular suffix).

The 'blessing' of Esau that follows in vv. 39-40 is, then, a negative blessing (Fokkelman: 'anti-blessing'). Verse 39 is a direct negation of v. 28 with a privative *min*,[3] and v. 40 reverses v. 29: 'you shall serve your brother'. Verse 40 again refers to a tribal context, and Esau is once more significant as the symbol of Edom in its shifting relations with Israel.[4]

Summary. The importance of Genesis 27 is that it separates Esau from his nearest family and, more precisely, his parents. (The separation

1.   Sternberg (*Poetics*, p. 55 [cf. pp. 164-65]) detects in the story a careful strategy aimed at splitting our sympathy between victim and victimizer.
2.   Cf. Skinner, *Genesis*, pp. 369-70.
3.   Cf. Westermann, *Genesis 12–36*, p. 539.
4.   Thompson ('Conflict Themes in the Jacob Narratives', p. 24) regards 27.46–28.9, together with 26.34, as a variant development of the Jacob story, which would originally have been independent and would have ended in Esau's threat to murder Jacob. In Thompson's view, this 'variant' (not 'source') tradition dealt mostly with Esau and the theme of national purity. I am not sure whether this view solves any problem—but it does generate one: the question of the existence of (more or less) independent Esau material.

from Jacob follows in chs. 32–33.) Technically, this happens by deceit and in the form of a negated blessing. In other words, ch. 27 corresponds to ch. 21 in the life of Ishmael. Both these chapters report the occasion of the definitive split between the first-born and his family.

In Genesis 27 the poetic sections containing Isaac's address (blessing/ anti-blessing) interrupt the narrative. This shows that the chapter is a combination of various traditional elements. Isaac's address reveals overt favouritism towards the fake Esau (and then the real Esau). But the one is blessed with success and fertililty, the other is denied both.

Genesis 32–33

Content and Composition. I have already dealt broadly with chs. 32–33, contrasting their general picture of Jacob and Esau with that in chs. 25 and 27. Here, I want first to examine some passages that may be deliberately intended to allude to the earlier chapters, and then to assess the position of these chapters in relation their present setting and to the other Esau/Edom sections.

Gen. 32.3 establishes the picture of Edom throughout this section. Living in Seir, in the country of Edom, he is primarily the Edomite overlord of his Israelite counterpart. We are informed of the number of his soldiers (400 men, 32.7; 33.1) and of the strategies that Jacob has to adopt to counter such a force. Jacob, miserably equipped for combat, clearly expects war and fears defeat. However, in ch. 33 Esau proves himself to be chivalrous and shows no intention of declaring war. This raises the question whether this passage preserves the memory of a meeting between Israelites and Edomites during Israel's desert wandering, as is suggested elsewhere in the Bible. I will return to this question below.

In their present shape the two chapters are clearly intended to form an appendix resolving the crisis in chs. 25 and 27. This raises the question of how, and from where, the story of the reunion developed. Skinner, Gunkel and Westermann, who represent traditional stances on this, all agree that 32.14(b)-22 formed one element in the composition of ch. 32. But while both Gunkel[1] and Skinner[2] ascribe it to E (together with vv. 2-3), Westermann[3] holds that J is responsible for

---

1. Cf. Gunkel, *Genesis*, p. 356.
2. Cf. Skinner, *Genesis*, p. 404.
3. Cf. Westermann, *Genesis 12–36*, p. 614.

the passage and allows no trace of E—although he admits that reliable criteria for an unambiguous separation of sources are absent from the chapter. While Gunkel and Skinner ascribe vv. 4-14a to J, Westermann explains these verses by segmenting them as follows: 4-8a, J; 8b-9, an etiological notice; 10-13, an expansion of the kernel in v. 12. Skinner, too, removes vv. 10-13 as a later expansion of J's narrative.[1] Gunkel also holds them to be secondary.[2]

For Genesis 33 the overall picture is clearer. Gunkel, Skinner and Westermann all argue for J provenance, Westermann for the entire chapter (vv. 1b-3 and 6-7 are pre-Yahwistic), and Gunkel and Skinner for all except parts of vv. 5, 10, 11 (and v. 4 and possibly 12-14 for Gunkel), behind which they discern the hand of E.[3]

In accordance with his structural approach to the Jacob Cycle, Fishbane regards Genesis 32 as the thematic counterpoint to 28.10-22. The connection between 32.2-8 and 28.11-17 has been noted and commented on by many others.[4] According to Fishbane, the common theme is 'encounter with the divine (beings) at sacred sites, near a border and accompanied by a *berakhah*'.[5] Correspondingly, Fishbane connects ch. 33 with 27.1–28.9, but in that case it is not solely the thematic repetition of chs. 27–28, but the complement. In chs. 27–28 the *bᵉrakâ* was stolen, now it is returned; in chs. 27–28 Jacob fled from the land, now he returns.[6]

Although Fishbane's observations are to the point, they do not, in my mind, properly account for what might be called the different 'modes of thought' in the complementary texts. Fishbane is insufficiently critical of the texts. Much the same holds true for Fokkelman's explications. He concentrates on key-words and follows the text consecutively (not in dichotomies, as Fishbane does), with frequent resort to concentric arrangements. But both still treat the figures of Jacob and Esau in Genesis 32–33 as individuals; the perspective is the same as for chs. 25 and 27. Everything that one needs to understand about

---

1. Cf. Skinner, *Genesis*, p. 406.
2. Cf. Gunkel, *Genesis*, p. 357.
3. Cf. Gunkel, *Genesis*, p. 365; Skinner, *Genesis*, p. 412; Westermann, *Genesis 12–36*, p. 638.
4. E.g. Westermann, *Genesis 12–36*, pp. 615-17; Fokkelman, *Narrative Art in Genesis*, p. 198; Blum, *Vätergeschichte*, p. 141.
5. Cf. Fishbane, *Text and Texture*, pp. 42, 53.
6. Cf. Fishbane, *Text and Texture*, pp. 42, 53.

the texts lies hidden in their structural arrangements. To lay bare the textual structure is both the key to the proper understanding of the narration, and the end result of the explanation! For all its merit, Fishbane's and Fokkelman's method lacks the dynamics of the traditio-historical approach. Even though statements on the finer distinctions between various sources tend to become routine and stereotypical, they often include many sharp observations on the texts. Discrepancies and 'oddities' in the text have to be explained even if one wishes to rebut the documentary hypothesis. In the case of Genesis 32, whereas most traditional scholars find vv. 10-13 to be alien to the 'original' context, Fishbane has nothing to say about them,[1] and Fokkelman thinks that they form the 'perfectly composed climax' to the scene (starting in v. 4).[2] On the other hand, mere source-critical ascriptions fail to do real justice to the important shift in attitude and milieu between chs. 32–33 and chs. 25 and 27 (although Gunkel, as noted above, is well aware of the matter).

In these circumstances, Blum's considerations of the literary units behind the present complexes are more rewarding. As noted earlier, Blum takes a reserved attitude to the subtleties of source-criticism, and he regards a separation of sources inside Genesis 32–33 as a violation of the narrative. The usual arguments for the separation are rejected on the ground that they rest on a failure to realize the demands of the narrative mode and the logical progress developed in the course of the narration. The various scenes and the recurring expressions create a coherent narrative continuity. Even the Penuel scene in 32.23-32 makes numerous references to the general context of ch. 32 and shows a degree of structural coherence that means that it cannot be isolated from the chapter as a whole (although he admits that vv. 24, 33 are later insertions).[3] Only for the inclusion of Jacob's prayer in 32.10-13 does Blum resort to the terminology of source-criticism (D).[4]

Chapter 32 forms the finale and summary of the Jacob story, full of thematic and contextual reptrospects to the Jacob–Esau and the Jacob–Laban complexes.[5] This concluding section also includes ch. 33, since the reunion scene clearly comes to an end in Gen. 33.16-17. Following

1. Cf. Fishbane, *Text and Texture*, pp. 53-55.
2. Cf. Fokkelman, *Narrative Art in Genesis*, p. 202.
3. Cf. Blum, *Vätergeschichte*, pp. 141-45.
4. Cf. Blum, *Vätergeschichte*, p. 158.
5. Cf. Blum, *Vätergeschichte*, p. 145.

Seeligmann, Blum calls 33.16-17 a formula of conclusion
('abschliessende Formel'): 'So X returned. . . and he called the
place. . .' (cf. Gen. 18.33; Num. 24.25; 1 Sam. 24.23; 26.25). The
whole episode of conflict and confrontation comes to an end at the
brothers' separation; Jacob belongs to Canaan, Esau to Seir.[1] So,
everything seems to indicate, in Blum's words, that 33.16-17 forms
the conclusion of one unit of tradition ('Überlieferungseinheit').[2]
What Blum means by this 'Überlieferungseinheit' is clear from the
following section of his book: 'the history of tradition of the Jacob-
story'. Far from being a composition of disparate sources, the Jacob
story is an independent narrative complex, a self-sufficient literary
unit ('eine in sich ruhende Texteinheit'). Ultimately, Blum's evaluation of the documentary hypothesis is that it is useless for explaining
the Jacob texts.

Unlike Fokkelman, Blum does not pass over the obvious differences
in relation to Genesis 25 and 27. He finds in chs. 32–33 an implicit
criticism of the Jacob's struggle for the birthright and blessing in chs.
25 and 27. In view of Blum's overall delineation of the background of
the Jacob story in the Northern kingdom of Israel and chs. 32–33 as
its finale, his explanation contains a major weakness. Why should a
confrontation between Jacob/Israel and Esau/Edom presented from a
Northern perspective have been depicted as peaceful?

Esau versus Jacob in Chapters 32–33. Throughout this section Esau
has the upper hand and Jacob goes out of his way to appease his
brother. Jacob's self-humiliation in front of Esau is conspicuous. He
addresses his brother with the words 'your servant' and 'my lord'
(compliments in glaring contradiction to the proclamation of 25.23)[3]
and asks, 'to find favour in your sight'. Jacob's rhetoric reaches its
climax in 33.10, when he likens the sight of Esau to seeing a god.
Fokkelman connects the verse with 32.31. Jacob's deliverance has been
from God and from Esau.[4] In my view, the parallel is not that evident.
In 32.27 it was the godlike figure itself, not Jacob, who asked, 'Let me
go'. However, Fokkelman is right to consider how, from the literary
style and language used in the section, the meeting between Jacob and

1. Cf. Blum, *Vätergeschichte*, p. 148.
2. Cf. Blum, *Vätergeschichte*, p. 149, and on the following, cf. pp. 147-50.
3. Cf. also Fokkelman, *Narrative Art in Genesis*, p. 200.
4. Cf. Fokkelman, *Narrative Art in Genesis*, p. 227.

Esau was conceived in the narrator's mind. In my view, 32.21 and
33.10-11 are particularly revealing of the author's understanding:

32.21

ואמרתם גם הנה
עבדך יעקב אחרינו כי־אמר
אכפרה פניו במנחה ההלכת לפני
ואחרי־כן אראה פניו אולי ישא פני

'And you shall say: "Moreover your
servant Jacob is behind us"'. For he
thought, 'I may *appease* him with the
present that goes before me, and
afterwards I shall *see his face*; perhaps he will *accept me*' (v. 20, RSV).

33.10-11

ויאמר יעקב אל־נא
אם־נא מצאתי חן בעיניך
ולקחת מנחתי מידי כי על־כן ראיתי
פניך כראת פני אלהים ותרצני

Jacob said, 'No, I pray you, if I have
found favour in your sight, then
accept my *present* from my hand, for
truly to *see your face is* like *seeing
the face* of God, with such favour
have you *received me*'.

קח־נא את־ברכתי אשר הבאת
לך כי־חנני אלהים וכי יש־לי־כל
ויפצר־בו ויקח

'*Accept*, I pray you, my *gift* that is
brought to you, because God has
dealt graciously with me, and because
I have enough.' Thus he urged him,
and he took it.

The terms used here—'appease [atone] him with a gift' [literally,
'appease his face'], 'see his face', 'accept me' [literally, lift up my face]',
'seeing the face of God'—are all idioms rooted in juridical-sacrificial
language. *kpr* (*piel*), denoting 'make atonement with', is seldom used
of dealings betweeen human beings as here. Compare Prov. 16.14,[1]
2 Sam. 21.3 and Num. 35.33, and also the saying in Prov. 6.34-35, a
warning against adultery, which is applicable to Jacob's situation and
illustrates the gloomy prospects for him:

> For jealousy makes a man furious, and he will not spare when he takes
> revenge. He will accept no compensation [*l' yś' pny kl-kpr*], nor be
> appeased though you multiply gifts.

The use of *kpr* in the Priestly literature, where it stands for a cultic
ritual performed by the priests (Lev. 9.22), is much more frequent.[2]

1. Cf. C. Westermann, *Genesis 12–36*, p. 622. Cf. also B. Lang, '*kippaer*',
ThWAT, IV, cols. 303-18 (310).
2. Cf. Lang, '*kippaer*', cols. 307-309.

Jacob's intention here is obviously to avert Esau's revenge,[1] by producing a gift as compensation. This gift is called *minḥâ*, rather than *kôper*, which would have been most appropriate here.[2] Thus, Jacob confesses himself to be the offending party and expects Esau to raise a case against him.[3] Jacob's intention is that 'his face' will be 'lifted up', in other words, that Esau's case against him will be withdrawn and that he will be accepted as his equal (and thus able to 'see the face' of Esau). The meaning of the expression 'to lift up somebody's face' in legal terminology is to 'favour or disfavour unjustly or partially', as for example, in Lev. 19.15:

> You shall do no injustice in judgment; you shall not be partial to the poor
> (*l' tś' pny dl*) or defer to the great.

The expression is also fairly frequent in the book of Job; see 34.17-19 (part of Elihu's speech):

> Shall one who hates justice govern?
> Will you condemn him who is righteous and mighty,
> who says to a king, 'Worthless one',
> and to nobles, 'Wicked man';
> who shows no partiality to princes (*l' nś' pny śrym*)
> nor regards the rich more than the poor. . . ?

The 'lifting up' of Jacob's 'face' appears in deliberate contrast with 'to see your face' and 'seeing the face of God' in Gen. 33.10. 'Seeing the face of God' is also cultic terminology (Ps. 42.3: 'when shall I come and behold the face of God?'), and Skinner's somewhat superficial interpretation of the 'flattering comparison' is that the words denote 'the feelings of joy and reverence with which one engages in the worship of God'.[4]

The 'present' of Gen. 33.10 is obviously the one planned by Jacob in 32.20. The language is ambiguous throughout and produces a double effect. Jacob's action is conceived of as an atonement in the juridical sense and symbolically as a sin-offering.[5] As Jacob makes atonement

1. Cf. Lang, '*kippaer*', cols. 310-11.
2. Cf. Lang, '*kippaer*', col. 316: a material satisfaction brought by the injuring party to the injured.
3. Cf. Bar-Efrat, *Narrative Art*, p. 67.
4. Cf. Skinner, *Genesis*, p. 414. Cf. also 1 Sam. 29.9; 2 Sam. 14.17; 19.28; but note that the comparison here is with 'the *angel* of God'.
5. Cf. Fishbane, *Text and Texture*, p. 52.

for himself before Esau, it is as though the act had been atoned for before God as well. (This idea is original to Gen. 32–33.) Jacob is aware of having brought guilt upon himself in the eyes of Esau and of God. It would be fully within Esau's rights to demand satisfaction from Jacob. The fact that he does not demand such satisfaction, and that only on Jacob's insistince is he willing to accept any, demonstrates the elevated tone of the narrative.

The two stories in Genesis 25 and 27 do not show Jacob suffering any pangs of remorse or guilt over what he and his mother have contrived (his hesitation in 27.12 is only because he fears failure). He pays for the birthright in ch. 25 like any other saleable commodity, and is satisfied with his mother's reassurances in 27.13. Esau's reaction in 27.41 is to plan to kill Jacob, but the reason for Esau's anger is the loss of his personal dignity in the eyes of Isaac. Esau, too, does not seem to realize the true nature of the offence as a violation of the birthright.

In Genesis 25 and 27 both Jacob and Esau merely act out their given roles, whereas in 32–33 they (Jacob in particular) are real personalities expressing complex feelings. Chapters 25 and 27 are the prerequisite to 32–33; the offender and the offended meet again and Jacob is able to return his 'blessing' (33.11: *qḥ-n' 't-brkty*) to Esau and so to make up for the blessing he had originally stolen.[1] The meeting is also theologically necessary as a corollary to 25 and 27. It was necessary for Jacob to find an opportunity to make atonement for his earlier offences. Only after Esau has been compensated is it possible for Jacob to part company with him and settle in Canaan (33.18). Like Abraham and Lot, Jacob and Esau part in peace; like Abraham, Jacob then settles in Canaan (cf. 13.12) and receives a renewal of the promise (13.14-18; 35.9-12).

Esau in Chapters 32–33. The difference between the descriptions of Esau and Jacob in these chapters and chs. 25 and 27 have been discussed above. In the earlier section a central theme was the conflict between the brothers; now it shifts to a meeting (though not of minds) and a resolution of conflicts. From Jacob's side, the reconciliation is conditional upon their subsequent separation; he is anxious not to give Esau any opportunity to remain within threatening distance (cf. 33.12-14).

1. Cf. Westermann, *Genesis 12–36*, p. 646.

Jacob is the necessary counterpart of Esau and there can be no question of any independent Esau-tradition behind Genesis 32–33. An interpretation of the chapters must take into account the significance of Jacob and Esau—both on an individual level, as personal antagonists, and on a symbolic level, as national representatives. These two levels need not be understood as different 'layers' combined to make up a 'story' (nor, indeed, as stemming from distinct sources), but together they represent the two facets of one Jacob–Esau story. More than anything else, the chapters amount to a theological evaluation of the history of the brothers' preceding lives. Jacob must once more encounter the shadows of his past before he is finally prepared for settling in Canaan, the land of the promise. Confronting his past in the figure of Esau, he turns first to God in prayer, and finally also addresses Esau as a 'godlike' creature. With this 'god' he has to wrestle once more, this time mentally, in order to achieve his 'blessing'. This he will achieve only if Esau accepts his gifts. For his part, Esau demonstrates his willingness to be reconciled to Jacob by accepting his gifts. The reconciliation is explained, as we have seen, in terms of an atonement.

On the symbolic level, Jacob and Esau represent the forces that lie behind them. Jacob is backed up by his family including many wives and concubines, children, cattle and possessions. This family represents all Israel as it was conceived in the author's mind: a nomadic group on the way to settling permanently in its own land and to becoming a nation. All come forward and prostrate themselves before Esau. Among Jacob's family, Joseph and Rachel are twice singled out for special mention (33.2, 7)—the image of a complete Israel.

The two levels cannot exist in isolation from each other. In drawing up plans against Esau and his forces (32.6-8), Jacob acts both in his own interest and in the interest of present and ensuing generations of Israelites. There is one passage, however, in which the symbolic level is virtually separate, Jacob's prayer in 32.10-13.[1] The prayer recalls and makes explicit Jacob's obligations as bearer of the promise and heir to the legacy of Abraham and Isaac. The fulfilment of the promise is now at stake, and with it Israel's future. It gives Jacob a strong case before God; it is God's concern, the God of Abraham and Isaac.

---

1. This is often regarded as an interpolation in its present context; so e.g. Westermann, *Genesis 12–36*, pp. 619-21. He takes the exclamation in v. 12 to be the original nucleus which was expanded by vv. 10, 11 and 13.

Overall, it is difficult to see how Genesis 32–33 could possibly belong to the same literary stratum (J) as 25 and 27. The theologically loaded language would have appealed to much later generations who saw their own situation as very different from that in pre-exilic times. In my opinion, the image of an Israel prostrated before Esau/Edom cannot easily be reconciled with the military achievements of Jeroboam I, as Blum suggests. In an attempt to find a place for chs. 32-33 within his theory, he poses the question whether the 'imperial claim to power' attested in Gen. 27.29, 40 would not have provoked a response (*Aufeinandersetzung*) from Northern Israel.[1] It is not completely clear to me which meaning is intended by the use of the word 'Auseinandersetzung' here, but Blum implies that chs. 32–33 can also be explained against the background of the early days of the Northern Israelite Kingdom.

Among Jacob's family, Rachel and Joseph are twice distinguished from the other members of Jacob's family who prostrate themselves before Esau. In my view this argues against Blum's notion of a Northern origin during Jeroboam's reign; surely this is a reign for which Joseph in humble prostration is not a good symbol. Chapter 33 signifies a confrontation between two potentially aggressive empires. Looking at it this way, the final settlement is reached more by mutual deterrence than by friendly reconciliation. Also from this point of view, Jacob's strategic manoeuvres ('that company of yours', 33.8) make a much greater impression on Esau than his gifts. Jacob's double tactics, simultaneously presenting his forces and his personal tribute, correspond effectively to the two levels of the story.

Now, the military consolidation of Jeroboam I after the break with the Southern Kingdom is not an obvious context for Genesis 32–33. These chapters' description of a reconciliation under pressure between the North (Israel) and the South (Edom) does not sit well with Blum's idea of an 'Auseinandersetzung'. Jeroboam's strategy was not appeasement or mobilization, but open religious provocation (1 Kgs 12.20-33).

S.H. Blank's solution is the complete opposite. The whole Jacob–Esau narrative in its present form should be viewed against a postexilic background. In Blank's view, the transformation of the significance of the original relationship between Jacob and Esau into one between nations is a very late phenomenon, as is the equation of Esau with

---

1. Cf. Blum, *Vätergeschichte*, p. 185. He agrees with the common view that Gen. 25.23b, 27.29a etc. refer to the submission of Edom under David (cf. p. 191).

Edom.[1] Blank's redating affects a whole chain of texts from Numbers 20 and Deuteronomy 2, to the prophetic statements on Edom. He connects the anti-Edomite utterances not with the events of 586 BC but with aggressive acts against Judah around 485, which would explain the growing exclusivism there after that date.[2] Many of Blank's suppositions and suggestions are justified, but others seem very strained.

What needs to be kept in mind is that chs. 32–33 provide the conclusion to the dealings between Jacob and Esau. On the individual level, it shows two contending brothers finally establishing peace between themselves. On the symbolic level, it is an episode of Israel's history explained in terms of the peaceful solution of an impending conflict. In recalling an original blood connection (33.9, 'āḥî) it echoes the Deuteronomic command in 23.8(7) not to abhor an Edomite, kî 'āḥîkā hû'. In fact, Genesis 33 may be a theological and ideological elaboration of such a statement in 'historical' terms. Genesis 25 and 27, with their stress on the conflict between individual brothers, could not have reflected a similar motivation. Genesis 33 and Deut. 23.8 seem to honour a common ideal of fraternal affection and benevolence.

Edom in the Old Testament. In order to fit the figure of Esau in Genesis 32–33 into a wider biblical frame, a brief survey of Edom in the Old Testament is necessary. Edom receives frequent attention in the Old Testament—only natural, in view of its location to the south of Judah (e.g. Num. 34.3; Josh. 15.1; 1 Kgs 9.26).[3] Accordingly, it is often mentioned together with the other neighbouring peoples in Transjordan, Moab and Ammon (e.g. Exod. 15.15; Isa. 11.14; Ezek. 25). The Edomites also had a reputation for wisdom (Jer. 49.7; Obad. 8).[4]

The Old Testament is aware of very early contacts between the Israelites and the Edomites. Numbers 20 tells how, during the Exodus, the Israelites are denied passage through Edomite territory on their way from Kadesh. The same event is alluded to in Judg. 11.17. Contrast this with their reaction to king Sihon the Amorite, whom they attack

1. Cf. Blank, 'Studies in Post-Exilic Universalism', pp. 182-83, 196.
2. Cf. Blank, 'Studies in Post-Exilic Universalism', pp. 185-86.
3. On the relationship between Judah and Seir/Edom, cf. Axelsson, *The Lord Rose up from Seir*, pp. 70-71.
4. Cf. M. Haller, 'Edom im Urteil der Propheten', in K. Budde (ed.), *Vom Alten Testament* (Festschrift Karl Marti; BZAW, 41; Giessen: Töpelmann, 1925), pp. 109-17 (110).

and conquer after he too denies them passage (Num. 21.21-26). Thus, both in Genesis 32–33 and Numbers 20 the imminent conflict is avoided, albeit by different means.

David's monarchy saw the beginning of a lengthy period of Edomite submission under Israelite dominion (2 Sam. 8.13 LXX; read 'Edom' for 'Aram' in the Hebrew; cf. also Ps. 60.2; 1 Chron. 18.12), interspersed by periods of Edomite revolt (1 Kgs 11.14-22; 2 Kgs 8.20) and reconquest (2 Kgs 14.7). On one occasion, Edom and Judah joined forces with the kings of Israel against King Mesha of Moab, their common enemy (2 Kgs 3). Among the Judaean kings, Amaziah and his son Uzziah conducted campaigns to re-establish and enlarge their rule over Edom. Judaean control ended with the coalition between Israel and Aram under Pekah and Rezin. This brought a welcome opportunity for Edom to free itself from Judah. 2 Kgs 16.5-6, in which the MT reads 'Aram', in all likelihood refers to Edom (cf. LXX v. 6, Ἰδουμαῖοι):[1]

> At that time the king of Edom recovered Elath for Edom, and drove the men of Judah from Elath; and the Edomites came to Elath, where they dwell to this day.

Later Edom became an Assyrian vassal state under Tighlath-Pileser III, and during the Babylonian incursion the Edomites took part in the plundering of Judah (2 Kgs 24.2).

Deuteronomy. The Deuteronomic/Deuteronomistic attitude towards Edom is very positive. I have already quoted Deut. 23.8(7), which rules that the Edomite, 'your brother', be let into the Assembly of the Lord. Chapter 2 reports how the children of Israel avoid conflict with their 'brothers, the children of Esau who live in Seir' (v. 48). Yahweh commands Israel not to provoke them; if they need anything from them they must pay for it. The description in Deuteronomy 2 refers to the same incidents during the Exodus as Numbers 20 (which was its source[2]), except that in Deuteronomy the Edomites are much more

---

1. Cf. the apparatus in *BHS*, commentaries *ad loc.*, and I. Avishur, 'Edom', *EncJud*, VI, pp. 370-77 (376). There is as similar confusion between Aram and Edom in 2 Sam. 8.13 (cf. above); 1 Kgs 9.26; 22.48; 2 Kgs 14.7, 22; 24.2.

2. Cf. A.D.H. Mayes, *Deuteronomy: Based on the Revised Standard Version* (NCB; Grand Rapids: Eerdmans; London: Marshall, Morgan & Scott, 1981), p. 135; Bartlett, *Edom and the Edomites*, p. 91.

favourably presented. There is no hint that Israel's passage through
their territory is or will be objectionable to them. Instead, it is implied
that the Edomites comply with Israel's wishes and grant them passage.
The prohibition on attacking the Edomites is theologically motivated
(as also with Moab and Ammon in the same chapter); the Edomites'
land is theirs by divine promise (Deut. 2.5, 9, 19). This represents a
rationalization of the conditions prevailing at the time of the author. If
Edom was not occupied, it must mean that they had never opposed
Israel, and Israel did not attack them because God had forbidden it.[1]
Conversely, compare Deut. 2.30:

> But Sihon the king of Heshbon would not let us pass by him; for the Lord
> your God hardened his spirit and made his heart obstinate, that he might
> give him into your hand, as at this day.

Deuteronomy explicitly states that Yahweh himself has secured possession of their land for the children of Esau. Verse 12 comments that
the descendants of Esau had taken possession of their country by
driving off the Horites, just as the Israelites did in their own land
'which Yahweh had given them'. The implication is that the two cases
are directly comparable. The comment continues in v. 22, in which
the standard set by Yahweh's dealings with Esau's children is applied
to the Ammonites:

> . . . as he did for the sons of Esau, who live in Seir, when he destroyed
> the Horites before them, and they dispossessed them, and settled in their
> stead even to this day.

Note the change of subject here. According to v. 12, the Edomites
themselves carried out the conquest; here it is Yahweh who has con-
quered for them. A similar reassurance is given to Esau's children in
Josh. 24.4: 'I [Yahweh] put Esau in possession of the hill country of
Seir'.

Now, if Yahweh had apportioned the region among the children of
Esau, Moab and Ammon (on the latter, cf. Deut. 2.9-10, 19-21) how
could Israel challenge Yahweh's decision by provoking those peoples?

The following three statements summarize the attitude taken to
Edom in Deuteronomy 2. Each of them could, theoretically, represent
a different phase in the construction of the chapter.

---

1. Following M. Noth, *Überlieferungsgeschichtliche Studien: Die sammelnden
und bearbeitenden Geschichtswerke im Alten Testament* (Tübingen: Max Niemeyer,
2nd edn, 1957), pp. 33-34.

1. Deut. 2.5: 'I have given the hill-country of Seir (RSV: Mount Seir) to Esau as a possession'. This would be the original expression of the Deuteronomistic idea of how the first Israelites had to proceed when they came into contact with the Edomites. It is restated in Josh. 24.4.
2. Verse 12: 'The Horites also lived in Seir formerly, but the sons of Esau dispossessed them, and destroyed them from before them, and settled in their stead; as Israel did to the land of their possession, which Yahweh gave to them'.[1]
3. Verse 22: '...as he did for the sons of Esau, who live in Seir, when he destroyed the Horites before them, and they dispossessed them, and settled in their stead even to this day'. This represents an elaborate evaluation and correction of v. 5.[2]

Deuteronomy 2, then, reflects a very positive attitude towards Edom which is necessary in order to account for Israel's failure to occupy Edomite territory. The same reasoning was probably later also applied to the case of Moab and Ammon. If the comparison of Moab and Ammon with Edom is not original to Deuteronomy 2,[3] then the pro-Edomite attitude would have originally been even more conspicuous. Edom's case would then have been unique among non-Israelites. The idea of Edom as 'chosen' must have had a considerable impact, since the insistence on an attitude of benevolence amounts to a volte-face in comparison to the violent reaction against Edom in the prophetic and poetic literature.[4]

The Prophets. The prophetic literature envisages a dreadful revenge to be carried out by Yahweh on the Edomites for their attack on Judah: 'slaughter in Edom' (Isa. 34.6); Yahweh's revenge (Isa. 34.8; Ezek. 25.12-13; Lam. 4.21-22); Yahweh's hatred (Mal. 1.2); Edom punished and devastated (Jer. 49.20-21; Ezek. 32.29; Joel 4.19; Obad. 6, 8, 9). Ezekiel is the strongest in this respect, and speaks of an 'eternal enmity' between Israel and Edom (35.5; cf. also 25.12-13; 32.29; 35.15; 36.5).

A total 'revolt' against a Deuteronomic-like attitude can be sensed in

1. Possibly part of an antiquarian notice; cf. Mayes, *Deuteronomy*, p. 137.
2. Cf. Mayes, *Deuteronomy*, p. 139.
3. So Mayes, *Deuteronomy*, pp. 136-38; vv. 9.10-12 does not represent the same tradition as v. 5.
4. Cf. Bartlett, *Edom and the Edomites*, pp. 92-93, who says that Deut. 2.5 counters the tradition of hostility; cf. also pp. 181-83.

Mal. 1.2-5, which reads as though it were taking to task the redactor(s) behind Deuteronomy 2 for their overfond attitude:

> 'I have loved you', says the Lord. But you say, 'How hast thou loved us?' 'Is not Esau Jacob's brother?' says the Lord. 'Yet I have loved Jacob but I have hated Esau; I have laid waste his hill country and left his heritage to jackals of the desert.' If Edom says, 'We are shattered but we will rebuild the ruins', the Lord of hosts says, 'They may build, but I will tear down, till they are called the wicked country, the people with whom the Lord is angry for ever'. Your own eyes shall see this, and you shall say, 'Great is the Lord, beyond the border of Israel!'

Although the impetus for this protest lies in the historical events behind the present circumstances, it is worded theologically. It is Yahweh's will to destroy the Edomites as a punishment for their treacherous conduct towards Israel. Indicative of the radical difference of attitude from Deuteronomy 2 is the use of the word 'brother' in v. 2. In Deut. 2.4, 8, 'brothers' is an epithet of 'the children of Esau who live in Seir', clearly a term of affection. In Mal. 1.2-5, on the other hand, the very fact of Esau's brotherhood is disputed by Yahweh himself and is converted into grim irony. 'Esau may well be Jacob's brother, but, as history will show, in reality I hated him!' Jacob and Esau have become prototypical objects for God's love and God's hatred in a way that cannot be explained by their individual roles in Genesis, but which becomes explicable in the light of Edom's role in the Babylonian conquest.

The epithet 'brothers' is used with varying nuances of meaning. Whereas in Malachi 1 it is ironic, in Amos 1.11 it is part of an accusation:

> Thus says Yahweh: 'For three transgressions of Edom, and for four, I will not revoke the punishment; because he pursued his brother with the sword, and cast off all pity, and his anger tore perpetually, and he kept his wrath for ever'.

This passage, commonly held to be postexilic,[1] fits well with Obad. 10, 12, where 'your brother' is also intended to bring out the gravity of Edom's crime:

---

1. E.g. H. Wolff, *Dodekapropheton. II. Joel und Amos* (BKAT 14/2; Neukirchen–Vluyn: Neukirchener Verlag, 1969), p. 194, etc. Contrast W. Rudolph, *Joel, Amos, Obadja, Jona: Mit einer Zeittafel von Alfred Jepsen* (KAT, 13/2; Gütersloh: Gerd Mohn, 1971), p. 134.

For the violence done to your brother Jacob, shame shall cover you, and you shall be cut off for ever (Obad. 10).

But you should not have gloated over the day of your brother in the days of his misfortune; you should not have rejoiced over the people of Judah in the day of their ruin; you should not have boasted in the day of distress (Obad. 12).

Classification of the Old Testament Passages. Old Testament statements on Edom may then be classified into separate groups according to whether the attitude taken towards Edom is positive, negative or neutral.[1]

Negative	Neutral	Positive
	Num. 21.4 (I)	
	Num. 33.37 (L)	
	Num. 34.3 (B)	
	Josh. 15.1 (B)	
	1 Kgs 9.26 (I)	
	2 Kgs 3.9 (union; Israel–Edom–Judah)	
	Jer. 40.11 (I)	
		Deut. 2.4-6 ('do not contend')
		Deut. 23.7-8 (RSV) ('do not abhor')
Exod. 15.15 (C)		
Num. 20.14-21		
(cf. Judg. 11.17) (C)		
1 Sam. 14.47 (C)		
2 Sam. 8.14 (C)		
2 Kgs 8.20 (C)		
2 Kgs 14.7 (C)		
2 Kgs 16.6 (read Edom) (C)		

1.   The various signs refer to the content of the passage:

B:	Outline of (Israel's) boundaries
C:	(Report on) confrontation Israel–Edom
I:	Information
L:	List
P:	Prayer for revenge on Edom
R:	Burden for Revenge

Negative	Neutral	Positive

Postexilic:
Isa. 11.14 (R)
2 Chron. 25.11-12 (C)
        28.17 (C)
Isa. 34.5-6 (R)
Jer. 9.25 (R)
     25.21 (R); cf. 27.3-11
     49.7-22 (R)
Ezek. 25.12-14 (R)
      32.29 (R)
      35.3-15 (R)
      36.5 (R)
Amos 1.11-12 (R); cf. 9.12
Obad. 1-14 (R)
Mal. 1.2-4 (R)
Joel 4.19 (R)
Lam. 4.21 (R)

                    Dan. 11.41 (I)

The upheaval of 587 BC clearly led to a turning-point in attitudes towards Edom. The pre-exilic passages give either information or lists in a neutral tone, or give reports on confrontations as a result of Edom's revolt and submission. In addition, there is the outspokenly favourable Deuteronomic view. National hatred between Edom and Israel seems to have been virtually unknown before the exile.[1] In the postexilic era the well-disposed attitude of Deuteronomy 2 and 23.8(7) has totally disappeared, replaced by condemnation, Dan. 11.41 being the only exception.

As I have already suggested, what triggered off this radical shift in attitude was Edom's behaviour during the Babylonian campaigns and especially during the last days of Judah's existence in 587. When they could have come to assist their own kin, the people of Edom instead joined with strangers and foreigners (Obad. 11-14), plundering and possibly even capturing and handing over the fleeing Zedekiah to the Babylonians (cf. Obad. 14 and 2 Kgs 25.1-7).[2] Esau/Edom, to whom, according to Deuteronomy 2, Yahweh himself gave their land, has become, by the exile, a mortal enemy. Consequently, Yahweh has

---

1. So Haller, 'Edom in Urteil der Propheten', p. 112.
2. Cf. J.D.W. Watts, *The Books of Joel, Obadiah, Jonah, Nahum, Habakkuk and Zephaniah* (CBC: Cambridge University Press, Cambridge, 1975), p. 59.

retracted his gift, so that Edom has finally become a 'realm of wicked-ness, a people whom Yahweh has cursed for ever' (Mal. 1). This pro-phetic voice was joined by others which also looked forward to the annihilation of the neighbouring peoples of Israel, heralding a new era of perpetual peace (Zech. 9).[1]

In the Ishmael section I concluded that questions of guilt and atone-ment were prominent in the period after the return from exile. Ezra–Nehemiah depicts the postexilic Jewish community as a penitent community (cf. above). The exile was the result of Israel's own sins. A similar religious background could well account for the language and tone of chs. 32–33 as well. On the moment of his return to his country Jacob has to face and make up for past iniquities. He is willing to 'confess' and 'make atonement' before Esau—and he still holds fast to God's promise to make his people numerous.

Confrontation in Genesis 32–33, Numbers 20 and Deuteronomy 2. A synopsis of the confrontation scenes in Gen. 32.4-5 (RSV: 3-4), 33.12-17, Num. 20.14-21 and Deut. 2.2-8 will help in further discerning the similaritites and differences:

G₁ (Genesis 32)	G₂ (Genesis 33)
And Jacob sent messengers before him to Esau his brother in the land of Seir, the country of Edom, instructing them, 'Thus you shall say to my lord Esau: "Thus says your servant Jacob. . ."'	Then Esau said: 'Let us journey on our way, and I will go before you'. But Jacob said to him: 'My lord knows that the children are frail, and that the flocks and herds giving suck are a care to me; if they are overdriven for one day, all the flocks will die. Let my Lord pass on before his servant, and I will lead on slowly, according to the pace of the cattle which are before me and according to the pace of the children, until I come to my Lord in Seir. So Esau said, 'Let me leave with you some of the men who are with me'. But he said, 'What need is there? Let me find favor in the sight of my Lord.' So Esau returned that day on his way to Seir. But Jacob journeyed to Succoth.

---

1. R.E. Wolfe ('The Editing of the Book of the Twelve', *ZAW* 53 [1935], pp. 90-129 [90, 95]) held this motif in the Twelve Prophets to represent one of several clearly definable strata, attributing these to individual editors; in this case 'the Anti-Neighbor Editor'. Cf. also Bartlett, *Edom and the Edomites*, p. 186.

N (Numbers 20)

Moses sent messengers from Kadesh to the King of Edom, 'Thus says your brother Israel: You know all the adversity that has befallen us; how our fathers went down to Egypt, and we dwelt in Egypt a long time; and the Egyptians dealt harshly with us. . . '
'Now let us pass through your land. We will not pass through field or vineyard, neither will we drink water from a well; we will go along the King's Highway, we will not turn aside to the right hand or the left, until we have passed through your territory.'
But Edom said to him, 'You shall not pass through, lest I come out with the sword against you'. And the people of Israel said to him, 'We will go up by the highway; and if we drink of your water, I and my cattle, then I will pay for it; let me only pass through on foot, nothing more'.
But he said, 'You shall not pass through'. And Edom came out against them with men, and with a strong force. Thus Edom refused to give Israel passage through his territory; so Israel turned away from him.

D (Deuteronomy 2)

Then the Lord said to me, 'You have been going about this mountain country long enough; turn northward. And command the people, "You are about to pass through the territory of your brethren the sons of Esau, who live in Seir; and they will be afraid of you. So take good heed; do not contend with them; for I will not give you any of their land, no, not so much as for the sole of the foot to tread on, because I have given Mount Seir to Esau as a possession. You shall purchase food from them for money, that you may eat; and you shall also buy water off them for money, that you may drink. For the Lord your God has blessed you in all the work of your hands; he knows your going through this great wilderness. . . " '
So we went on, away from our brethren the sons of Esau who live in Seir, away from the Arabah road from Elath and Ezion-geber.

All these passages report a confrontation between Jacob/Israel and Esau/Edom. The terminology is not consistent except in G$_2$: Jacob and Esau. In N the parties are 'the children of Israel' and 'Edom'; and in D 'we' and 'the children of Esau'. The confrontation ends in a clear separation between the two.

Comparing these texts, G$_1$ and N both open with a messenger formula: Jacob and Moses send messengers to Esau and Edom respectively. This element is lacking in G$_2$, in which Jacob and Esau communicate face to face. In D it is Yahweh who commissions a messenger. In its present arrangement G$_1$ describes a preliminary contact, probing Esau's intentions, before the actual meeting in Genesis 33. It is not a request for passage. Jacob is the approaching party here, as is Israel in N and D.

Between G_2 and N, the role of 'challenger' is reversed. In G_2 Esau performs the part, and it is he who 'says' (33.12, 15) and Jacob who 'answers' (13, 15). Jacob makes every effort to ward off Esau's approach; he even declines Esau's offer of a troop to escort him and his company. In N, Israel is the intruder and initiates the exchange of messages, 'So says your brother' (Num. 20.14), which Edom answers (v. 18). The dialogue continues in vv. 19 ('the Israelites said') and 20 ('and he [Edom] said'), until finally Israel withdraws and takes another route (v. 21). Also, whereas Jacob's only weapon in G_2 is his ingenuity, Edom in N puts all its men under arms. The result, however, is the same in both passages: the challenger/intruder retreats.

The main difference between N and D is that in D the whole middle section (the dialogue in G and N) is missing (Yahweh is the formal spokeman in D as Moses is in N), and only the narrative frame remains: right of passage is requested, granted and takes place. No reaction from 'the children of Esau' is recorded; it is implied, however, that permission is granted and Israel is able to pass through. By omitting the exchange of requests and refusals in relation to N, an image is created of a fully harmonious relationship between Israel and Esau/Edom.

The lacuna in D makes a comparison between G_2 and D unrewarding, since the dialogue in the latter forms the basis for understanding the outcome of the former. Another point of difference is also clear, namely that G_2 is very aware of a potentially dangerous rivalry between Jacob and Esau, while D shows no such awareness, or ignores the rivalry by its harmonization-through-omission. In this sense, G_2 stands between N and D, since the conflict is not carried to the brink of open hostilities as in N, but neither is it denied or ignored. On the other hand, Esau's first suggestion in G_2, to escort Jacob to his destination, is unthinkable in both N and D.

D has, as mentioned earlier, reasons of its own for giving the Edom passage a particular slant. D is clearly secondary in relation to N, and both N and D evidently represent a tradition that differs from the one behind G_2. The latter, though independent of both N and D, seems to be related to them, if only remotely, recalling as it does an almost ceremonial meeting between Esau and Jacob. It is possible that a tradition about a meeting between Israel and Edom formed the nucleus of Genesis 32–33, and that the same tradition was reinterpreted under the new conditions of the postexilic age.

G_2 contains a variant of the dialogue section in G_1, but lacks an introductory phrase that would set the scene; it merely continues the scene set already in 33.4, where Esau and Jacob embrace affectionately. G_1 establishes the contact and is clearly the version in line with the opening of N and D, whereas G_2 contains the concluding separation element which is absent from G_1. Accordingly, G_1 and G_2 together formally correspond to N and D, 32.3 and 33.16 forming the frame within which the reunion takes place. This frame may be borrowed from N (or the tradition behind it), but it is in any case augmented with the protracted negotiations between Jacob and Esau.

Thus, the story in Genesis 32–33 seems to be a retrojection back to the life of Jacob and Esau of conclusions reached by much later theologians sanctioning the inevitable accommodations made with postexilic conditions. The author's awareness of differing national qualities guided the presentation of the meeting between the alienated patriarchs. One of them is on his way back to the country of his birth; the other is heading for a foreign land and is associated with another nation.

Conclusions. The above survey of the shifting biblical stances toward Esau/Edom shows that Genesis 32–33 belongs to a totally different milieu from the outbursts in the prophets.[1] The presentation of Jacob and Esau as equals (at least at the moment of their reunion) is not compatible with these harshly condemnatory oracles. The circles behind Genesis 32–33 either knew nothing about the aggression against Israel that incited the prophets, hence the chapters are pre-exilic, or they wanted to mitigate its effect. Nor does anything in the story hint of the prospective downfall of Edom. Instead, Esau is glorified and venerated by Jacob. In a postexilic setting this is comprehensible only if the author(s) were deliberately trying to instil an attitude towards

1. Dicou (*Jakob en Esau*, pp. 186-88) advances the thesis that the role of Esau/Edom is one and the same in Genesis and the Prophets: the antitype of Jacob–Israel and an archetype of Israel's enemies. My point against him would be that Genesis (Dicou does not consider Deuteronomy) already contains a twofold presentation of Esau. The Prophets certainly oscillate between the real, concrete Edom and the archetype, as Dicou also notes (pp. 82-83). Edom's identity as a 'nation' was probably absorbed by the 'type' through a gradual process connected with historical changes. What survived was an image of Edom as the typification of evil which could also be absolutized to take on an apocalyptic dimension. So also, broadly, Haller, 'Edom im Urteil der Propheten', pp. 115-17. In other respects Dicou reasons along very similar lines to myself.

'Esau/Edom' at odds with the prevailing hopes of revenge.

On the other hand, Genesis 32–33 is also clearly of a very different character from Deuteronomy 2. There is an almost tangible tension in the air when Jacob and Esau meet. This tension is evident in Jacob's precautionary steps before the meeting and his ruses to impress Esau. Deuteronomy 2 understands the boundaries of Edom to be clear-cut, given by divine order and inviolable by Israel. Israel's portion was Canaan and Genesis 33 is similarly aware that Seir was Esau's alloted territory (vv. 16, 18). But in Genesis 32–33 Esau is still a potential aggressor, although he is turned back by Jacob's shrewdness. This may be understood as a bow to the 'traditional' enmity between Edom and Judah. For its part, Numbers 20 depicts an Edomite reaction that is explicitly and outspokenly hostile.

Summary. My contention is that the author(s) of Genesis 32–33 applied the pattern of the confrontation in Numbers 20 to the lifetime of Jacob and Esau, the forefathers of their respective nations. The author already knew that the previous confrontation between Edom and Israel had ended without warfare. So, by analogy, the confrontation between Jacob and Esau must have been resolved peacefully, even if Jacob did prepare for the worst. The author's explanation for this would be that a reconciliation between Israel and Edom had already taken place in their forefather's days, thanks to Jacob's meticulous endeavours to bring about atonement.[1] The result was already a given: separation, Esau giving way to Jacob.[2] This explanation differs from that in Deuteronomy 2, since the settling of the conflict did not come about by Yahweh's prescription, but was worked out by Jacob. In this respect, Genesis 32–33 and Deuteronomy 2 represent divergent (even competing) positions.

Like Deuteronomy 2, Genesis 32–33 must also have been 'theologically' motivated. It is difficult to specify any historical milieu for its origin other than that of the postexilic Jewish community of the resettle-

1. Jacob willingly brings 'offerings' as though to a god. Such conduct cannot be linked to any worship of Edomite gods. 2 Chron. 25.14 is in all likelihood unhistorical and serves the need to find a cause for Amaziah's defeat by Jehoash of Israel. The author was at home in Priestly circles and naturally chose the means of atonement between Jacob and Esau from his surroundings.

2. Cf. Westermann, *Genesis 12–36*, p. 642. I do not, however, subscribe to Westermann's psychologization of the author's intentions.

ment. Yet, as we have seen, in contrast to the picture of their relationship in Genesis, historically the relationship between Israel/Judah and Edom was mostly one of violent confrontation, culminating in the destruction of both kingdoms.

I am unwilling to place Genesis 32–33 within an early Northern-Israelite framework. A 'programmatic' interest may indeed lie behind the present chapters, but it is concerned with efforts at consolidation much later than those of Jeroboam, King of Israel. Instead, I submit that it was the reconsiderations forced upon the postexilic community that influenced the final editing of the chapters.[1] The new conditions that faced the community included the necessity of working out a *modus vivendi* in relation to foreigners. In contrast to the prophetic texts, Genesis 32–33 pursues a more moderate line, endorsing an attitude of integration and reserved openness. The chapters may possibly contain a covert criticism of the prophetic outrage. Yet it should also be noted that the meeting of Jacob and Esau ends in their final separation.

Esau's Marriages

Esau married three wives: two Hittite women (of different families), Judith and Basemath (Gen. 26.34), and then the daughter of Ishmael (28.6-9). (Compare this with his $tōl^edôt$ in ch. 36, which represent a different tradition;[2] only the number, not the names, are the same as before.) The marriage to Ishmael's daughter is presented as a move on Esau's part to propitiate his father Isaac after his previous mistake in marrying the Hittite women. Furthermore, Esau's departure to Ishmael (28.9) is a deliberate move to counter Jacob's journey to Laban in quest of a wife. Esau receives as wife a first cousin on his father's side, Jacob one from his mother's side. The true lineage is guaranteed here by an alliance with the mother's family (and on the mother's initiative). By choosing 'women of the land', Esau has already dissociated himself from Rebecca (cf. Ishmael and his Egyptian alliance). Now he distances himself still further from her and from what is to become the Jacob–Israel family by marrying a daughter of the expelled Ishmael.

---

1. Dicou (*Jakob en Esau*) also hints at a similar background for the Jacob story; cf. the English summary, p. 298.
2. Cf. also Blum, *Vätergeschichte*, p. 449.

Chapter 4

THE GENEALOGICAL LISTS OF ISHMAEL AND ESAU

Contexts (Genesis 25 and 36)

The two genealogical lists of Ishmael and Esau beginning in Gen. 25.12 and 36.9 refer to *tōlᵉdôt* in conformity with other texts of similar · character. The one extant Ishmael-list in 25.12-18 is much shorter than the Esau-list in 36.4-14. Moreover, for Esau there are two additional lists in ch. 36: vv. 15-19 and 40-43. The Ishmael list is evidently an intrusion into a context that forges a link between Abraham's death and the life of Isaac. But otherwise it is held together as a unit. In the case of Esau, the insertion of several lists has brought about considerable confusion over the context of ch. 36 and has split it into small fragments.[1] These are clumsily linked together, as is shown by the reiteration of the statement that Esau was the ancestor of the Edomites; it occurs first in vv. 1 and 8, introducing and concluding the passage on Esau's wives and children, then again in v. 9 and finally in vv. 19 and 43.

'Twelve' is the number of Ishmael's sons, his 'princes' (25.16). The total of Esau's sons and grandsons by his three wives (excluding Amalek) can also be figured as twelve, so it is possible that the twelve tribes of Israel stood as a model for him as well.[2]

'Types' of Genealogical Lists in Genesis

The Ishmael and Esau genealogies must not, of course, be treated in isolation from other similar lists in Genesis. The extant genealogical lists in Genesis conform to two types:

1. Gunkel (*Genesis*, p. 389) gives seven divisions.
2. So Skinner, *Genesis*, p. 431.

1. A type where the main interest is in binding together many generations, by registering the names of several (as many as possible) father–son successions. It is often headlined *tōlᵉdôt* and rounded off with the summary, 'These are the sons of NN, in their lands, each with his own language, by their families, in their nations', or some similar phrase. This type in turn would appear in two forms:

   1a. A 'forward-looking' type that takes heed of the father's *posterity* and lists his *descendants*. It *begins* with the first father and is 'horizontally' oriented in that the name of the father is given first and then those of all his sons, generation by generation. In this way, each generation is grouped together.

   1b. A 'backward-looking' type that traces the *ancestry* of the father in question. Accordingly, it *ends* with his name, and it is 'vertically' oriented in the sense that one specific line of succession is drawn through many generations.[1] The lineage is followed back to the 'beginning', ideally Adam or Noah. In addition, the age of each individual member of the clan is noted at the birth of the next member, and the total number of his years at the time of his death.[2]

2. A 'biographical' type, which remarks on a great feat on the part of the hero (e.g. a founder of culture: 'he built a city', Gen. 4.17).[3] It may also have the character of a 'birth narrative'.[4]

---

1. Cf. the characterization of the Cainite genealogy as 'linear' in form by M.D. Johnson, *The Purpose of the Biblical Genealogies with Special Reference to the Setting of the Genealogies of Jesus* (SNTSMS, 8; Cambridge: Cambridge University Press, 1969), p. 7. Wilson's terms 'segmented genealogy' and 'linear genealogy' also correspond broadly to my 'types' 1a and 1b respectively; cf. R.R. Wilson, *Genealogy and History in the Biblical World* (Yale Near Eastern Researches, 7; New Haven: Yale University Press, 1977), pp. 196-97.

2. A similar distinction to the one here between 'vertically' and 'horizontally' oriented genealogies is recognized by C. Westermann (*Genesis 1–11* [BKAT, 1/1; Neukirchen–Vluyn: Neukirchener Verlag, 1974], p. 13), but within the J genealogies.

3. Westermann (*Genesis 1–11*, p. 16) holds such information to reflect expansions (one of several types) of the 'original' genealogy (see the previous note).

4. Wilson, *Genealogy and History*, p. 146, for 4.17-26; cf. also pp. 147-49, for his argument concerning 'genealogy and narrative'. He suggests that names to

The two types may be illustrated by some examples. For 1a, we may cite Gen. 10.1-31, the generations of the sons of Noah:

> These are the generations of the sons of Noah, Shem, Ham, and Japheth . . .
>
> The sons of Japheth: Gomer, Magog, Madai, Javan, Tubal, Meschech, and Tiras.
> The sons of Gomer: Ashkenaz, Riphath, and Togarmah.
> The sons of Javan: Elishah, Tarshish, Kittim, and Dodanim. (From these the coastland peoples spread.)
> [These are the sons of Japheth] in their lands, each with his own language, by their families, in their nations.[1]
> The sons of Ham: Cush, Mizraim, Put, and Canaan.
> The sons of Cush: Seba, Havilah, Sabtah, Ra'amah, and Sabteca.
> The sons of Ra'amah: Sheba and Dedan.
>   . . .
> (20) These are the sons of Ham, by their families, their languages, their lands, and their nations.
>   . . .
> The sons of Shem: Elam, Asshur, Arpachshad, Lud, and Aram.
> The sons of Aram: Uz, Hul, Gether, and Mash.
>   . . .
> (31) These are the sons of Shem, by their families, their languages, their lands, and their nations.

What is aimed at here is as complete a list as possible of each single generation descended from Japheth, Ham and Shem. In fact, however, the list is complete only for the second post-diluvian generation.[2] After that generation, individual lineages seem to be chosen at random. The core of the list is the idea of the post-diluvian diffusion of the peoples of the earth and their common ancestry from a hero in existing tradition.[3]

which biographical notices are attached—such as Enoch—were originally contained in separate traditions. On 'culture founders' in Wilson's Near Eastern material, cf. pp. 149-55. He concludes that the genealogical aspect is not essential in Gen. 4.

1.   The bracketed words are supplied by RSV from vv. 20 and 31.

2.   See also the table in Westermann, *Genesis 1–11*, p. 667. Westermann argues mainly on the basis of the conventional source critical approach to the genealogies, and discerns in ch. 10 a blend of J and P; cf. also pp. 13-15, 670, and, on the genealogies in general and their sociological background, pp. 8-11.

3.   Cf. Skinner's comparative table of divergencies between different versions (*Genesis*, p. 233).

As an example of 1b, the 'vertical' list in 11.10 is another record of Shem's descendents:

> These are the descendants (*tôl^edôt*) of Shem.
> When Shem was a hundred years old, he begot Arpachshad two years
>   after the flood;
> and Shem lived after the birth of Arpachshad five hundred years, and had
>   other sons and daughters.
> When Arpachshad had lived thirty five years, he begot Shelah . . .

One particular line of descent is followed here, down to Terah and Abram in v. 26: Shelah–Eber–Peleg–Reu–Serug–Nahor–Terah. The function of this type is clear: to trace the pedigree of Abram, the protagonist of the following section. In Gen. 5.3-32, the descent of Noah is similarly established and derived from Adam (v. 1; cf. also the genealogy of Jesus in Matthew and Luke).

Finally, type 2 is found in Gen. 4.17-26[1] and also in 11.27-29.

In practice, the 'types' are not kept strictly apart, and elements from more than one type may appear in combination, as in 10.1-32 (vv. 8-12 clearly belong to type 2):

> Cush became the father of Nimrod; he was the first on earth to be a
> mighty man. He was a mighty hunter before Yahweh; therefore it is said,
> 'Like Nimrod a mighty hunter before Yahweh. . . '

That vv. 8-12 represents an alien corpus within the larger framework beginning at v. 1 is clear from v. 7 which had already listed the sons and grandsons of Cush. Verses 8-19 have apparently been appended from another list.

The various 'types' of genealogies suggested here should be judged to be of different origin. However, the types defy any attempts to define their sources. Traditionally, scholars allocate the above 'types' to J or P, but Gunkel, for example, also speaks of 'two different traditions, not harmonized by P',[2] as an explanation of why Arpachshad in 10.22 is only the third son of Shem, whereas in 11.12 (and 10.24?) he is the first-born. Westermann distinguishes between J and P genealogies, but he qualifies this with numerous expansions.[3] For M.D. Johnson the division of the material according to separate sources is the key organizing

---

1. Cf. Johnson, *The Purpose of the Biblical Genealogies*, p. 8.
2. Cf. Gunkel, *Genesis*, p. 156.
3. Cf. Westermann, *Genesis 1–11*, pp. 13-16.

principle for his treatment of all the genealogies in the Pentateuch.[1]
Wilson too regards the Yahwist as responsible for 4.17-26.[2]

From my view-point the divergent list types need not be explained
primarily on the basis of different sources, but on the basis of different
interests. The standard considerations of age and character of the
classic sources cannot easily be demonstrated within a genealogical
list. Formal differences in genealogies seem instead to depend more
on sociological function than on adherence to a specific source. If a
list shows a mixed character, that is because its function dictated the
use of material from different types.

Lists of various 'types' may have been compiled for a wide range of
purposes, as suggested by Johnson,[3] so that, for example, when an
ancestor's lineage was demanded, one particular type of genealogy,
looking backward, would be provided. For ch. 10 and Gunkel's
'unharmonized traditions', I prefer an explanation that concentrates on
the *function* of the different types—mainly 1a, with minor sections
from 1b (8a, 24) and 2 (2, 8b-12). As Wilson[4] points out, we do not
possess first-hand knowledge of oral genealogies in Israelite society.
He himself resorts to comparative anthropological data and distinguishes between three functions for oral genealogies: domestic, politico-
juridical and religious.[5]

1. Cf. Johnson, *The Purpose of the Biblical Genealogies*, pp. 3-6. For the
Cainite genealogy in ch. 4, however, he confesses that it must have been a more or
less self-contained unit originally (cf. p. 10). For the P material he assumes the existence of a separate Toledoth-source within the P corpus proper (cf. p. 16).

2. Cf. Wilson, *Genealogy and History*, p. 144; cf. also the discussion (139-
41). Indeed, it is interesting to note that Wilson, who is generally critical of the previous source-critical approaches (cf. p. 11), nonetheless discusses the biblical material
in literary categories; hence the use of the words 'sources' and 'gloss' regarding
Gen. 4.17, and the 'original text' and so on; cf. pp. 139, 140-41, etc.

3. Cf. Johnson, *The Purpose of the Biblical Genealogies*, p. 4: 'Classification
of Semitic tribes around Palestine'; cf. also pp. 26-29.

4. Cf. Wilson, *Genealogy and History*, p. 12.

5. Cf. Wilson, *Genealogy and History*, pp. 131-6, 18-20, 37-40. Note especially his statement (p. 54). 'The purpose of the recital [of genealogies] is not to provide the sort of accurate historical account that is the goal of the modern historian but
to legitimize contemporary lineage configurations. A genealogcial list may, however,
contain reliable data, although that has to be decided on an individual case-basis'
(italics mine); cf. also p. 55.

The Ishmael and Esau Lists

The different interests associated with the various 'types' above can also be checked against the Ishmael and Esau lists. As far as the former is concerned, one would expect that the intention would have been to relate him and his sons to other tribes and peoples of later generations—in other words a 1a type. Gen. 25.12 ($tōl^ed\hat{o}t$) to 16 meets such expectations precisely. The sections of v. 16 ('villages', 'encampments', 'tribes') correspond directly to 'lands', 'languages', 'families' and 'nations' in ch. 10. Gen. 25.17, on the other hand, is not part of the genealogy, but sums up the life of Ishmael by announcing the number of his years and his burial, after the pattern of similar phrases on Abraham (25.7-8). It is verse 18a that is the immediate continuation of 16 and which defines the area inhabited by the sons of Ishmael (note the plural which is abandoned in 18b). This can be compared with, for example, 10.19. Accordingly, 25.17 is not at home in this context and was probably interpolated in order to complete the biography of Ishmael.

For Esau in ch. 36, the picture is more complicated. The chapter comprises seven major units, a fact that naturally gives an impression of disunity.[1] A 1a type begins in v. 9 ($tōl^ed\hat{o}t$) and ends in 14. The descendants of Esau are grouped around his three wives, exactly like Jacob's sons in the previous chapter:[2]

> by Adah: Eliphaz: Teman, Omar, Zepho, Gatam, Kenaz
> by Basemath: Reuel: Nahath, Zerah, Shammah, Mizzah
> by Oholibamah: Jeush, Jalam, Korah

Another list follows in Gen. 36.15-19 that names 'the chiefs' of the sons of Esau (*'allûpê* as against $n^es\hat{i}'im$ for the 'princes' of Ishmael in 25.16). This list does not fully harmonize with the previous one: Korah and Amalek (in v. 12 the latter was the son of a concubine) are

---

1. Wilson (*Genealogy and History*, p. 173) nonetheless finds 'a definite formal structure' in the arrangement of the genealogies. By this he means a 'redactional unity' (p. 174). He discerns different functions for the various genealogies, in the political, geographical and social spheres. The genealogies may well have been in use during the same historical period, and all may originate from the same source; cf. pp. 179-81. On this chapter, cf. also Bartlett, *Edom and the Edomites*, pp. 86-87.

2. Cf. Skinner, *Genesis*, p. 431; Wilson, *Genealogy and History*, pp. 168-69.

now sons of Adah.[1] The sons of Basemath and Oholibamah are the same, including Korah. It would seem, therefore, that Gen. 36.17 and 18 were copied from the first list,[2] whereas vv. 15-16 were taken from an original 'short-list' of the chiefs, with the intention of retaining the number 12 arrived at if Amalek and the 'extra' Korah are removed. This list, then, would represent a modified 1a type, with secondary additions.

Two more lists tracing Esau's genealogy still remain in the chapter (36.1-5): Esau's wives and their origin (2-3), and Esau's sons by each wife (4-5). The names accord fully with vv. 9-14, except that here no grandchildren are recorded. It is a collocation of data about Esau's family affairs, although the names of the women diverge from those in 26.34 and 28.6, as previously noted. Such divergences suggest that vv. 1-5 have undergone a secondary harmonization with the other sections in the chapter,[3] and that they were prefixed to the whole chapter as a buffer between the lists and the earlier records of Esau's marriages. Therefore, these verses cannot represent any primary 'type' of list.

Likewise, 36.40-43 cannot represent any 'pure' type of genealogy;[4] rather, they should be viewed as an appendix[5] to the lists of the kings of Edom in vv. 31-39.[6] Pointing to the names which are at least partly inconsistent with those in 15-19, Gunkel regards these verses as

1. Cf. also Wilson, *Genealogy and History*, p. 178.
2. Westermann (*Genesis 12–36*, p. 687) thinks that vv. 15-19 developed from 11-14.
3. So also Wilson, *Genealogy and History*, p. 174, who finds here one of several instances of 'genealogical fluidity' in the chapter. Other instances concern the name of Oholibama and the overall arrangement of the various genealogies; cf. pp. 176-78. Westermann (*Genesis 12–36*, p. 684) holds the names to be taken (by P) from vv. 9-14.
4. Cf. Wilson, *Genealogy and History*, p. 173.
5. So also Westermann, *Genesis 12–36*, p. 689: 'Anhang'.
6. Verses 31-39 are commonly considered to be ancient, from Edomite sources, perhaps annals of administrative districts accessible to Israelite court officials after the conquest. Skinner's view of these verses is similar, following some remarks on their P style (cf. *Genesis*, p. 436). Westermann (*Genesis 12–36*, pp. 683-84) takes the verses to be a list of Edomite kings coming from the royal chancery in Edom and transferred to Jersualem after the conquest; cf. also Axelsson, *The Lord Rose up from Seir*, p. 67. R.H. Pfeiffer's suggestion of a separate 'S' source of Edomite origin (cf. *Introduction to the Old Testament* [New York: Harper Bros., 1941], pp. 159-61) has not received much scholarly support.

composed on the basis of the earlier list and of no historical value.[1]
Another possibility would be to explain the discrepancies as traceable
to separate processes of transmission; so for example, the different
number of names could reflect a shifting administrative organization.
These verses were evidently in accord with the Chronicler's knowledge and so were included in 1 Chron. 1.43-50.

The sundry lists are interrupted by a brief narrative section in
Gen. 36.6-8 about the separation between the two brothers. In contrast
to the earlier separations between Jacob and Esau, when the reasons
were defeat (25.34), treachery (27.43) or marriage (28.5), the reason
given here is completely neutral: the land did not have the capacity to
feed both brothers' herds.[2] This clearly happens in imitation of the
separation between Abram and Lot.[3] Like Abram in 12.5, Esau has
become wealthy, but chooses (without the encouragement that Abram
receives in 13.9) to leave the land of Canaan and settle in another
country, 'away from his brother Jacob'. The section evidently purports to be the 'final' report of the separation; now Esau is a nation of
his own, and Jacob can have Canaan for himself.

Summary

The genealogical material about Ishmael and Esau can be viewed as
evidence of an intense interest in their lineage, and their consanguity
with Isaac and Jacob. It was in the interest of later generations to
follow up that relationship by drawing the ancestral line further, in
order to relate present conditions and contemporary tribes to tradition. The genealogical lists stand as the culmination of such interest.
The various types of lists outlined above ultimately served the need to
organize the peoples and territories of the surrounding world. The
lists exhibit the belief that the organization of the world and its
peoples was instituted by God and served the divine plan for Israel.

1. Cf. Gunkel, *Genesis*, p. 394.
2. Cf. also Thompson, *The Origin Tradition of Ancient Israel*, p. 114.
3. Cf. also Westermann, *Genesis 12–36*, p. 685.

Chapter 5

THE REUBEN TEXTS

Moving from Ishmael and Esau to the case of Reuben means shifting from an extra-Israelite to an inner-Israelite context. Reuben is the first-born of Jacob, the eldest of his sons, and thus he belongs within the 'Israel' of the twelve tribes. The etymology of his name given in Gen. 29.32 (on the basis of *'ny*, 'pain', together with the obvious verb *r'h*, 'see', 'see, a son!')[1] is too simple to be taken seriously. It is obviously secondary. Also the *r' šyt 'wny*, 'the firstling of my vigour' of Gen. 49.3 is probably meant as an allusion to the name, as regularly occurs in such 'blessings'.

The title 'first-born', *bkwr*, is repeatedly appended to Reuben's name: he is called the first-born of Jacob in Gen. 35.22, 46.8 and 49.3, and of Israel (in various lists) in Exod. 6.14, Num. 1.20, 26.5 and 1 Chron. 5.1, 3. In view of the challenge posed by Judah and Joseph to Reuben's position among the twelve, one would expect Reuben's birthright to have been 'problematized' much sooner than in 1 Chron. 5.1, 3. On the other hand, 'first-born' is omitted in passages such as Exod. 1.2 and 1 Chron. 2.1 where one might have expected it to appear.

There is a twofold image of Reuben in the Bible. In Genesis he is a distinct individual appearing in larger narrative contexts; but from Exodus onwards, his name only appears as part of a collective, the tribe.

Reuben in Genesis

The texts in Genesis involving Reuben are: 30.14-16; 35.22; 37.19-25, 29-30; 42.21-22, 37. Reuben appears in Genesis in two contexts. In one he is involved in two incidents from which his brothers are absent. In 30.14-16 he is accompanied by Jacob's two wives, Rachel and Leah. It is a story with strong erotic overtones, in which Leah acquires access

---

1.   Cf. Westermann, *Genesis 12–36*, p. 577.

to her husband from Rachel in exchange for the mandrakes which her son Reuben has gathered.[1] Leah's access to Jacob happens through Reuben, and although on one level the story is about the contest between the two wives for the same husband ('wasn't it enough that you took away my husband...?'), symbolically it also describes the role of the first-born in relation to his mother: he is proof of her ability to fulfil her prime duty in providing offspring. In her husband's eyes, her primary asset is her first-born son. From this aspect, Reuben's gift of the mandrakes to Rachel also implies a kind of remission of the first-born: he is exchanged for access to the father.

The story in Gen. 35.22 is a total reverse of this: now he acts on behalf of his father. The affair with Bilhah may be taken to symbolize not only the first-born as the prime proof of his father's procreative power (Gen. 49.3), but also his role as guarantor of its continuation in ensuing generations. In that respect, the Bilhah episode presents Reuben as a repesentative of his father.

While Gen. 35.22 keeps up a totally matter-of-fact tone and does not elaborate on any possible breach of moral principles in the story, Gen. 49.3-4 clearly conveys reproof. The allusion to 35.22 here is possibly not original;[2] *hll* (*piel*), 'to profane', 'defile', is a term belonging to the cultic-legal sphere and thus is probably an an interpolation in this context. Gen. 49.4 is the only instance of the word in this particular sense within the whole of Genesis.[3] However, in 1 Chron. 5.1-2 the moral is drawn and the consequences for Reuben are stated in full: Reuben's birthright and status has been transferred to Joseph *because of* his violation of his father's bed. Gen. 49.4 is quoted almost verbatim: *bᵉhallᵉlô yᵉṣûʿê ʾābîw* (1 Chron. 5.1). Its efforts at harmonization make this passage an early midrash on Gen. 35.22. It presupposes, first and foremost, an awareness of the historical realities that had brought Judah and Jerusalem to the center of Israel's continued existence, while at the same time leaving the biblical tradition

1. On 'mandrakes' (traditional reading of *dwd'ym*; LXX: μῆλα μανδραγορῶν), cf. K. Schneider and E. Stemplinger, 'Alraun', *RAC*, I, pp. 307-10 (307-308).

2. C. Westermann (*Genesis 37–50* [BKAT, 1/3; Neukirchen–Vluyn: Neukirchener Verlag, 1982], p. 255) suggests that the extant oracle on Reuben is secondary. An original saying would have been expanded by linking it to 35.22.

3. It appears 3 times in Exodus, 19 in Leviticus, 2 in Numbers and 3 in Deuteronomy—as against 30 in Ezekiel! What is 'defiled' in Gen. 49.3-4 is Jacob's marital status; cf. W. Dommershausen, 'חלל *hll* I', *ThWAT*, II, cols. 972-81 (980).

about Reuben's primogeniture intact.[1] In addition, the passage implies a clear conception of individual guilt and responsibility for one's actions (cf. 1 Chron. 21.8).

On the other hand, in the Joseph complex (Gen. 37) he appears as the defender of a younger brother.[2] It is Reuben who saves Joseph's life in 37.21-22 by suggesting that the lad be cast into a pit—and so concealing his intention to restore him to his father later on. As an individual he proves himself to be more compassionate than the others and is fully vindicated in 42.21-22 when his brothers bitterly repent selling Joseph. In this section Reuben stands out against the other brothers who remain an anonymous group. Reuben acts as his brothers' spokesman before Jacob (42.37) and is accountable to him for Joseph. He is also Jacob's representative to his brothers.

All this changes, however, when Judah replaces Reuben as spokesman before Jacob (43.3-5, 8-10) and before Joseph (44.16, 18-34).[3] Within the narrative complex of chs. 43–44, Judah supersedes Reuben. Chapter 42 acknowledges Reuben's position as first-born, while in ch. 43 he seems to be completely forgotten. However, in contrast to the cases of Ishmael–Isaac and Jacob–Esau, the 'conflict' between Reuben and Judah remains hidden throughout Genesis. Its existence is never openly recognized and no confrontation is reported. Not even in ch. 37 is there any real competition; always when one of the two makes his appearance the other somehow vanishes or remains silent:

> 19-21 They [Joseph's brothers as a group] speak, Reuben answers [dialogue]. Judah is silent: 'They said to each other, "Look, the dreamer is coming. . . let us kill him. . . " And Reuben heard . . . and said, "Let us not take his life".

> 22 Reuben speaking 'to them' [monologue; Judah silent]:
> 'Let us not shed blood. Throw him into this pit, but do not lay hands on him.'

---

1.   J.M. Myers, *1 Chronicles: Introduction, Translation and Notes* (AB; New York: Doubleday, 1965), p. 35. Contrast G. Brin, 'The Birthright of the Sons of Jacob', *Tarbiz* 48 (1978–79) (Hebrew), pp. 1-8 (5), who regards passages such as 'his birthright was given to the sons of Joseph' and 'the birthright belonged to Joseph', as incorporating an old tradition that the Chronicler used (a tradition possibly similar to that lying behind Gen. 48.22 and LXX 2 Sam. 19. 44).

2.   Cf. Berlin, *Poetics and Interpretation*, p. 121.

3.   Cf. Westermann, *Genesis 37–50*, pp. 127, 130; cf. also 32-33. He suggests a narrative 'sequence' rather than a doublet.

24 They throw him into the pit

26-27 Judah speaking 'to his brothers' [monologue; Reuben absent (cf. 29)]: 'What shall we gain by killing our brother . . . Let us not lay hands on him . . . And his brothers obeyed ["heard"] him'.

29 Reuben returns

Notwithstanding A. Berlin's argument to the contrary,[1] the cracks in this construct are still immediately striking. For example, why should Judah suddenly revive the idea of killing Joseph once it has been called off by Reuben's intervention (v. 24)? and where does Reuben go to?[2] To me it seems clear that the writer/editor has made little effort to remove the tensions here. He simply could not see the real nature of the conflict between Reuben and Judah over Joseph. And since it never came to any open clash or dispute between them (in the style of chs. 17, 21, 25, or even 48) there could be no resolution, whether by divine declaration (17.20-21) or oracle (25.23), or patriarchal decree (27.39-40; 48.20). The same applies to ch. 42 as to 43: when one appears, the other disappears.

This shows that even at the time of the integration of the Joseph cycle into Genesis the question of Reuben's and Judah's status was still unsettled, and it was left to later commentators, the contributor of Gen. 49.4 and the Chronicler to sort out the matter. And for the latter the conflict concerns not two but three protagonists: Reuben, Judah and Joseph—the one around whom the fraternal strife evolved in the first place. This happens because the latent conflict in Genesis is not between tribal representatives—as in 1 Chron. 5.1-2, where it becomes a national-religious problem (as indicated above).

Reuben in Other Books

As stated above, from Exodus onwards Reuben's individuality disappears and his name survives only in tribal nomenclature: 'the sons of Reuben' (e.g. Gen. 46.9; Exod. 6.14; Num. 1.20; 7.30; 16.1; 26.5; Josh. 4.12; 13.23; 22.9; two grandsons in Deut. 11.6); 'the tribe [*mṭh*]

---

1.   In favour of a unified literary work, by appeal to 'artistic ingenuity and integrity', cf. *Poetics and Interpretation*, pp. 120-21. Cf. also Alter, *The Art of Biblical Narrative*, pp. 166-67.

2.   The Ishmaelite–Midianite issue may not cause serious trouble in view of the discussion above; cf. Berlin, *Poetics and Interpretation*, pp. 119-20.

of Reuben (e.g. Num. 1.21; 13.4; Josh. 20.8; cf. 1 Chron. 6.48, 63); 'the camp [*mhnh*] of Reuben' (Num. 2.10, 16; 10.18); 'the clans [*plgwt*] of Reuben' (the Song of Deborah, Judg. 5.15-16); and with the gentilic ending, 'Reubenites' (e.g. Deut. 3.12; 29.7; Josh. 1.12; 12.6; cf. e.g. 1 Chron. 5.6). These are fairly evenly distributed among the Pentateuchal books, although Numbers exhibits the greatest variation and includes instances of all the terms listed. Joshua and 1 Chronicles also vary between several terms, although omitting *mhnh*. Deuteronomy is more restricted, lacking both 'the children [plural]' (in contrast to the frequent 'children of Israel', 'children of Levi' and the like) and 'the tribe'. The *plgwt* of Judges 5 is not used elsewhere.[1] Besides these, compounds of these terms may be used, for instance, 'the tribe of the sons of Reuben' (Josh. 13.15) and 'the tribe of the Reubenite children' (Num. 34.14). 'Reuben' alone may also denote the whole tribe, as in Deut. 27.13 and 33.6; likewise, 'Reubenite' in 4.43.

In no way do these texts down-play Reuben's primogeniture. Reuben is constantly the *bkwr*. The word functions in the above cases as a kind of title justifying, for example, the order of a list of the tribes and the allotment of the land among the sons of Jacob. The Reubenites are also assigned a leading role in the occupation of the land: Joshua commands them to cross the River Jordan 'before your brethren', together with the Gadites and the half-tribe of Manasseh (e.g. Josh. 1.14; 4.12)—Reuben's neighbours in Transjordan.

Evidently, as long as the perspective of the twelve tribes is preserved, the Reubenites take a prominent position, notably in Joshua. The Deuteronomistic conception of the conquest as the concern of all Israel under the leadership of Joshua required the participation of Reuben and the other settlers of Transjordan. (In Num. 32.20-27, the Reubenites' wish to settle there is interpreted by Moses as a lack of solidarity with Israel, and he consents only on the condition that they first join their fellow tribes in the battle for the western territories.)

A more reserved attitude is taken in Judg. 5.15-16, where, like Gilead, Dan and Asher, Reuben is chided for failing to join his kinsmen under Deborah: 'Why did you tarry among the sheepfolds, to hear the piping of the flocks?'[2] Far from being eager to rush to the

---

1. Cf. F.M. Cross, 'Reuben, First-Born of Jacob', *ZAW* 100 (1988), pp. 46-65 (49).

2. Differently Cross, 'Reuben, First-Born of Jacob', p. 48: 'Thou indeed hast dwelt among the hearths. . .', taking *lmh* as an emphatic plus enclitic. Cross sees in

battlefield, Reuben prefers a less turbulent life among his flocks. Neither does the Song of Deborah contain any allusion to Reuben's primogeniture.

So, the biblical sources clearly support Reuben's status as the first-born of Jacob, and some efforts are required on the part of the Chronicler to strip him of that rank, efforts that have a strong flavour of harmonization and rationalization. The Chronicler is also the one who fills in the lacunae left by other records, by providing a consistent end to the history of Reuben and his nearest kinsmen: in retribution for their idolatry, they are exiled by Tiglath-Pileser (1 Chron. 5.26).[1]

Summary

In summary, Reuben only appears as an individual in Genesis, and even the presentation of his character is perplexingly two-sided. He is the principled brother as well as the delinquent son.[2] The common thread between Genesis and the rest of the Bible is Reuben's primogeniture, which is universally recognised; even the Chronicler, who is anxious to deprive him of his birthright, preserves the epithet. There is no story about Reuben's loss of his birthright (Gen. 35.22 in itself carries no such implication). In this his case differs from that of Ishmael and Esau. For Reuben there was no divine instigation to effect or sanction the reversal of his status. It was left open for subsequent reflection to draw conclusions about cause and effect, and, accordingly, 1 Chron. 5.1-2 offers not a story but a theological rationale: Reuben himself had forfeited his birthright. Applying the law of sin and retribution made any other divine intervention redundant.

these verses evidence that Reuben was flourishing in the twelfth century BCE. He assigns to Reuben a major role in the formation of Israelite society, of religious as well as political importance. The strategic position of his area would have opened up the way for the 'Moses-group' coming from Midian into Canaan, and he also refers to events known to have taken place in Reubenite territory, assuming the existence of a sanctuary of Yahweh in the valley opposite Bet Pe'or; cf. pp. 50-55, 60-61.

1.   The Mesha Inscription (c. 830 BCE) does not mention Reuben and would indicate that by then Reubenite territory had already been diminished by Moabite incursions: 'I made the highway in the Arnon valley. . .' For the whole text in translation, see *ANET*, pp. 320-21. The actual disappearance of the tribe of Reuben is lost in history, and what evidence remains offers only indirect clues for tracing the process.

2.   Cf. Berlin, *Poetics and Interpretation*, p. 119.

Chapter 6

THE MANASSEH TEXTS

Ephraim and Manasseh form the last link in the chain of brother-pairs studied here. Two texts in Genesis involve the two sons of Joseph: 41.50-52 and 48.5, 8-20.

Genesis 41.50-52

41.50-52 is an isolated passage clumsily forced into the context of Joseph's successful arrangements to avert the famine in Egypt.[1] It records the names of Jospeh's two sons born to him in Egypt (46.27), and also the name of their Egyptian mother of priestly descent. Customary etymologies follow the name-giving, and they indicate that Joseph understands the birth of his sons as recompense for earlier losses: 'God has made me forget (*nšny*) all my hardship', and 'God has made me fruitful (*hprny*)[2] in the land of my affliction'. The same theme appears elsewhere in the Joseph complex—in 50.20, for example.

Genesis 48.5

Gen. 48.5 is part of a larger section beginning from v. 1, where Joseph visits his father on his sick-bed and hears him uttering words of blessing. In v. 5 Jacob adopts Joseph's two sons as his own, 'as Reuben and Simeon are'. The adoption (Westermann prefers legitimation)[3] is

1. Westermann (*Genesis 37–50*, p. 101) thinks that the verses rightly belong together with the Jacob story as its conclusion.
2. Cf. also Gen. 49.22. The etymology is evidently not taken account of by J.C.H. Lebram, 'Jakob segnet Josephs Söhne: Darstellungen von Genesis XLVIII', *OTS* 15 (1969), pp. 145-169 (164).
3. That is, of Ephraim and Manasseh as independent tribes; cf. Westermann, *Genesis 37–50*, p. 208, and Sternberg, *Poetics*, p. 353. Differently I. Mendelsohn,

motivated in 48.7 by the death and burial of Rachel near Ephrath
(35.19). Thus, the adoption too is intended to make up for a loss, not
of any other sons of Jacob, but of Joseph's mother. In addition, the
author behind the section explicitly connects Manasseh and Ephraim
with Reuben and Simeon, which suggests that the former are viewed
as compensation for disappearance/dispersion of the latter. Ephraim
and Manasseh accordingly fill the gap left by three earlier losses.

Genesis 48.8-20

In vv. 8-20 Joseph's two sons are again, strangely enough, complete
strangers to Jacob, who shows no awareness of the adoption act in the
preceding verses. Joseph has to introduce them anew. This passage can
be broken down into the following subsections:[1]

A	8-12		Joseph introduces his sons to Jacob
B	13-14, 17-20		Jacob blesses Ephraim and Manasseh
	B.1	13-14	Ephraim and Manasseh are brought before Jacob
	B.2	17-18	Joseph reproves Jacob
	B.3	19	Jacob's insistence
	B.4	20a	The blessing
	B.5	20b	Evaluation: Jacob put Ephraim before Manasseh
C	15-16		Jacob blesses Joseph

C is obviously misplaced in its present position, since it clearly interrupts the narration.

The main theme of vv. 8-20 is blessing, of Joseph and of his sons.
The first blessing, in v. 15, is termed a blessing of Joseph (anticipating
ch. 49: 'he blessed Joseph'), but in the actual wording of the blessing
God is called upon to 'bless the lads'.[2] Verses 15-16 are probably
secondary incorporations into the context. In fact, they would fit in
much better with vv. 1-7 after the adoption: 'in them let my name be
perpetuated, and the name of my fathers . . .'

Apart from this, the context in Gen. 48.8-20 is concerned with the

---

'A Ugaritic Parallel to the Adoption of Ephraim and Manasseh', *IEJ* 9 (1959–60),
pp. 180-82, who found the verse to contain 'precise Babylonian terminology' and
also compared it with the Hammurabi Code, §170 (on which see the Ishmael section).

1. Cf. Westermann's 'Segensritual' (*Genesis 37–50*, p. 210).

2. Westermann (*Genesis 37–50*, p. 212) suggests that a blessing of Joseph did
originally belong to vv. 15-16.

relative status of Manasseh and Ephraim.[1] It is Jacob who reverses their status by transferring the dignity of the primogeniture from Manasseh to Ephraim. By crossing his arms as he lays his hands on the boys' heads, he indicates with his right hand that Ephraim is the one to whom the first-born's blessing should belong. From an historiographical point of view, this is a device with which to bestow the authority of Jacob the patriarch, sanctioning Ephraim's position as a historical entity within the ideological framework of 'the land'. 'Ephraim' is of course here identical with a specific part of that land.[2] From a literary point of view the most interesting feature is the ingenuity of the author in producing yet another variation on the theme of the reversal of the first-born's status. This time, as in the case of Jacob and Esau, and less analogously, Reuben, it is the aging patriarch's blessing that decides the birthright. However, there is no element of deception here; on the contrary, the patriarch himself makes his preference known, and in a very ostentatious manner. The scene is already prepared for in 48.13 with Joseph approaching Jacob leading one of his sons by each hand. Jacob's final 'verdict' is underscored by Joseph's irritation over his father's clear demonstration of his intentions, and his counter-move to have the blessing 'correctly' administered. Jacob's act of blessing is clearly seen by Joseph (and the author) as a deviation from the convention for blessing the first-born. (Compare this with Rebecca's precautions in ch. 27 to convince Isaac that the first to be blessed really was Esau, and Isaac's question to the same end.) Indeed, the story makes a great play of the deviation—it is for all to see that Jacob places Ephraim first.

The order of the blessing corresponds to its wording: 'God make you like Ephraim and Manasseh'. It seems, however, that the wording itself does not imply that Manasseh will lose his position to Ephraim. That is only made clear by the following comment, 'Thus he put Ephraim before Manasseh'. The 'blessing' is explicitly said to have had a proverbial status among the Israelites: 'God make you like Ephraim and Manasseh'.[3] It seems very likely that it is only here— adapted to its present setting, put in Jacob's mouth, and followed by

1.   So also Westermann, *Genesis 37–50*, p. 213.
2.   Cf. Westermann, *Genesis 37–50*, p. 215, on the aetiological character of the passage.
3.   Westermann (*Genesis 37–50*, p. 216) regards it as an old tribal saying and compares it with 12.3b; 18.18; etc.; as such it was added to the *Mehrungsverheissung*.

the appropriate comment—that the saying could have any bearing on the relative status of the brothers. By itself, the saying 'God make you like Ephraim and Manasseh' communicates nothing more than a wish that God may make the addressee successful; as successful, that is, as both Ephraim and Manasseh already are.

In fact, it is the promise of many descendants in 48.19 that lays down the real standard of comparison for Ephraim's priority:

> He said, 'He [Manasseh] also shall become a nation and he also shall be great, but his younger brother shall be greater than he and his seed shall become a multitude of nations'.

According to Num. 1.32, 35, the numbers of Ephraim's descendants are not remarkably higher than those of Manasseh, but that is not the essential thing here. What is essential is the fact that by these words Manasseh is ranked in the category of 'second-comers', together with Ishmael and Esau (17.20; 21.13; 25.23). The intention in all these cases is to justify, after the event, the ascendancy of the younger brother.

Thus the section purports to find a justification for the process that led to the establishment of 'Ephraim' as the leading tribe in Israel's history. Ephraim's sovereignty, it contends, was initiated by Jacob; its 'dynasty' had patriarchal sanction. His status relative to Manasseh is, by comparison, of minor importance, and may only have had relevancy as a reflection of factional rivalries in the Northern Kingdom. That a pattern with implications for all Israel was applied to Ephraim and Manasseh shows that the author was looking for an organizing principle that could make sense theologically as well as historically. In consequence, the *motif* may be secondary in this case.

Summary

I noted that the three textual units on Manasseh–Ephraim are isolated, and that the only text of some length (Gen. 48.8-20) has a composite character. It contains a double blessing, the first of which (vv. 15-16) seems to be at variance with its immediate context and may be a secondary addition from another context, possibly vv. 1-7. The second blessing, in v. 20, is built around a proverbial saying, in this instance used to underpin the demotion of Manasseh and the elevation of Ephraim. Verse 20 is the logical culmination of vv. 13-14, 17-18 . The section purports to explain and authorize the rise to power of the half-tribe of Ephraim.

Chapter 7

CONCLUSIONS

My aim in this final chapter is to draw together the earlier sections under two viewpoints: what *formal* features do the texts have in common (the textual perspective), and what *thematic* features (the thematic perspective) do they share? The conclusions drawn from such a survey should also reveal something about the interplay between these texts and the larger framework in which they were placed. This will give an insight into the historical *Sitz im Leben* for the motif.

The Textual Perspective

Some further observations must be made concerning links between the texts already studied. Sternberg[1] mentions serialization as a device for acquiring cumulative force in biblical narrative. This is certainly relevant to the first-born motif.[2] The descending series of older brothers is accentuated by its very repetition in the narrative complex of Genesis. On the other hand, from a formal and structural point of view it is the *differences* between the texts, rather than the features they have in common, that immediately stand out. Possible similarities have to be searched for. For the Ishmael and Esau complexes one may point to the sequence of oracle–birth stories involving a confrontation with the older brother and notes on their future lot. Both Ishmael and Esau are also explicitly designated as becoming 'a [great] people'. For Ishmael the designation comes from Yahweh himself as a promise to his mother, recurring not less than three times (Gen. 17.20; 21.13, 18; four if 16.10 is included). For Esau it is proclaimed in the oracle, 25.23. In this way Ishmael and Esau are linked together:[3] they will share in a

---

1. Cf. Sternberg, *Poetics*, pp. 109-11.
2. Cf. Sternberg, *Poetics*, p. 113.
3. Compare also the marriage between their children.

similar future. But a certain similarity in their biographical outline must not obscure the important differences in their respective stories.

For Manasseh and Reuben, Genesis affords a minimum of biographical information apart from announcing their birth. Manasseh is granted a promise of numerous descendants (*Mehrungsverheissung*, 48.19) as was Ishmael; and, like Esau and Manasseh, Reuben is graced with a solemn blessing, an expression of the patriarch's last will (49.3-4). For all three of them, the hour of blessing (including the divine reassurance to Ishmael through Hagar) simultaneously brings with it the final renunciation. After that decisive confrontation, the first-borns are 'the forsaken' and from then on they have only to fulfil the future prescribed for them. The decision is communicated in different ways. Esau is openly declared a *persona non grata* in his father's house in much harsher words than those used for the demotion of Manasseh. However, for all practical purposes, the outcome is the same for both: Jacob's blessing portends an inferior rank for them in relation to the ancestors of Israel. Ishmael, Esau and Reuben also have in common their association with a concubine or 'women of the land' (while no effort is spared to ensure an appropriate match for their counterpart). Thereby, they threaten to subvert the original intention of the call of Abraham,[1] and the 'blessings' are evidently meant to abort this threat. In these instances the blessing is really an act of dissociation *from* the 'blessed'. This applies also to the 'blessing of Reuben' in its present form, Gen. 49.3-4. The expression *'l twtr*—insofar as its meaning can be correctly ascertained—and Yahweh's proclamation to Abraham concerning Ishmael (17.20, 'I will *bless* him') both carry a similar implication: the loss of pre-eminence. Thus the principle of 'blessing' is what comes nearest to a common denominator for all the texts. In every case the 'blessing' signals the formal announcement of the demotion of the first-born. It is spoken by an authoritative voice (Yahweh, a patriarch) and recorded as a direct quotation.[2] In effect it removes the protagonists from the patronage of their own family.

---

1. Cf. Sternberg, *Poetics*, p. 134. Some of Reuben's brothers were sons of concubines (Bilhah and Zilpah), but they are kept within the family by associating them with the mistresses of their mothers, Rachel and Leah.

2. Cf. Sternberg's consideration of God's direct statement as fulfilling both a performative and an anticipatory role: God's speech is a creative act (*Poetics*, p. 106). *Mutatis mutandis*, this applies also to the patriarchs' declarations to Esau, Reuben and Manasseh.

The Thematic Perspective

Sternberg also points to the Bible's partiality for representing God's choice as a determining factor in Israel's history, leaving little or no room for further elucidation—such *faits accomplis* as God's choice of Noah, Abraham and Joseph.[1] One aspect of this is the rejection of the first-born of the three great ancestors. Each generation heralds a new edition, as it were, of the act of election. This election, that is, God's choice, seems to pass both unchallenged and unmotivated. Only for Reuben is the motive for exclusion inquired after, and then more vaguely in Genesis 49 than in 1 Chronicles 5. This process of exclusion is subsequent to and dependent on the promise to the Fathers, which is likewise repeated for each generation (Gen. 12.1-3; 26.24; 32.9-12). Hence, Ishmael and Esau will beget 'peoples', described in relation to one of the patriarchs (cf. Gen. 21.13, 'because he [Ishmael] is your [Abraham's] seed').

The Relevance of the Motif

An inquriy into the relevance of the motif of the forsaken first-born within the narrative context of Genesis is, I believe, better pursued in terms of its 'meaning' than by speculations about its origin. The textual analyses have pointed in two directions: first, to the *geographical* and *national* relevance, which is clear. Under this aspect, the motif is part of the narrative strategy in Genesis to lay out the formation of the nations and races on earth under the auspices of the God of Israel. The books of the Pentateuch are very conscious indeed of the existence of foreign peoples. From Exodus onwards these are mostly peoples with whom the children of Israel come into some sort of contact— encounters during the desert wandering, war and so on. In Genesis, however, there is another dimension: a systematic interest in purely numerical matters under which lies an idea of how the world's peoples proliferated and spread within pre-ordained boundaries. Assorted tribes and races, peoples known and unknown, are paraded in lists, registers

---

1. Cf. Sternberg, *Poetics*, pp. 98-99; on the first-born motif, cf. esp. 183-84. Cf. also R.S. Hendel, *The Epic of the Patriarch: The Jacob Cycle and the Narrative Traditions of Canaan and Israel* (HSM, 42; Atlanta: Scholars Press, 1987), pp. 111-16.

and tables interspersed throughout the larger narrative sequence. Much of this material has probably been added by later hands; traditional source criticism assigns much of this material to P. It betrays the concern to include as many peoples as possible and to allocate to each nation a specific place in space and time. Some of the peoples concerned obviously had closer contacts with Israel than others and may have maintained quite close relationships with them.

Secondly, the motif has a *theological relevance*. Theoretically, the lists and tables in Genesis present a series of options for God's inscrutable and immutable decisions. But none of them require any further elucidation except the very final one, the choice between the two or more children of each great ancestor. For Jacob and Esau, Reuben and Judah, and Ephraim and Manasseh, the choice itself is delegated to the father of the latest generation.[1] Effectively, however, on these occasions they act as representatives of God. Their preferences are implicitly God's as well. In this way the motif of the Forsaken First-born may be said to underline Israel's consciousness of its own standing as God's elected people. In this way also, Israel's self-consciousness[2] as a separate nation—its election—found expression.

A *Historical* Sitz im Leben *for the Motif*

A historical situation in which both the national and theological relevance would have been clear is that of the postexilic Jewish community, reassembled after the turmoils of the sixth century and slowly regaining its strength. Amidst foreign powers and nations, it had to rebuild an identity for itself. As we have seen, these endeavours could take an exclusive course, one utilizing segregation to define the 'true' Israel. The ultimate goal would have been to ensure survival by preserving the highest degree of national 'purity'. Under such circumstances the community could naturally turn to the standards and paradigms set forth in history and tradition, including the stories of the patriarchs and their dealings in changing situations. (Compare the early church and the life of Jesus.) From this aspect, Abraham's attitude to Hagar and her son could be interpreted as exclusivist.[3]

1. Jacob, the last patriarch, also blesses Joseph's children.
2. Cf. Smith, *The Religion of the Landless*, p. 197: 'a self-conscious community that is occupied with self-preservation'.
3. In his study on the separation motif in the *Book of Jubilees*, E. Schwarz

However, it is also possible to trace an inclusive line of thought, one of integration and of accepting foreign influence and influx into Judah and early Judaism. This course is already heralded by Deutero-Isaiah and later by Trito-Isaiah, who welcomes proselytes into the Assembly of Yahweh (Isa. 56.3-7). The Priestly edition of the book of Genesis shows a similar tendency in its universalist ramifications. In my view, the promise that Ishmael will become 'a people also' is best understood against such a background. A similar background could well lie behind the editors of, for example, Genesis 32–33. The story is both a corrective and a covert criticism of the vindictive attitude of the Prophets and Psalms towards Esau. The implied author of these texts seems ready to say, 'Now the time of revenge has passed, now is time for reconciliation; we can afford to be cooperative as long as we are allowed to keep within our own boundaries and preserve our own identity intact!'

It seems also that the 'blessings' of the first-born sons are worked out in deliberate reference to the concept of God's election of Israel. Yahweh himself reassures Abraham, 'I will make Ishmael a people also'. In this way, God's choice is not challenged, but supplemented, by adding an idea of 'also-peoples' to the chain of 'also-sons' in the patriarchal narratives. In addition, the scope of the stories themselves is broadened to take in the experiences of the postexilic circles who demonstrated an active interest in the world around Judah. Their

---

traced its roots to the prohibition against making a covenant with 'the peoples' (Exod. 23.32; 34.12.15; Deut. 7.2; Judg. 2.2), and he also allocated the conception of Israel's identity in Jubilees within the same ideological frame. However, 'identity' as framed by our texts is more limited than Schwarz's conception of it. His approach is traditio-historical and allows one and the same concept to be instanced on a diachronic scale from several different periods of Israel's history; cf. Schwarz, *Identität durch Abgrenzung*, pp. 13-14, 61, 149. In my perception, it was only through the challenges of the exilic and, in particular, the postexilic period that the 'technicalities' of a reaction to foreign influence come to the fore. In the past, Israel could at least be conceived of (forbidding what is not conceivable makes no sense) as a negotiating party on a bilateral basis, that is, conceived of as able in some sense to regulate its own position and relations to foreign powers (cf. the covenant principle). In the period following upon the exile, Israel by contrast was hardly able, for the foreseeable future, to vindicate such a status for itself vis-à-vis others. What the community of Israel could do then was to turn backwards and inwards, to contemplate the standards and paradigms set forth by its own history and traditions, and apply them to the contemporary situation.

experience of recent historical changes had taught that 'also-peoples' outside the tiny area of Judah had some standing in God's plans. Such 'also-peoples' were linked with the antecedents of Israel by the discovery (not the invention) of the potential of God's promises to the Fathers: 'I will make the son of the maid into a people also, because he is your seed'.

BIBLIOGRAPHY

Alter, R., *The Art of Biblical Narrative* (London: Allen & Unwin, 1981).

—'A Literary Approach to the Bible', *Commentary* 60 (1975), pp. 70-77.

Avishur, I., 'Edom', *EncJud*, VI, pp. 370-77.

Axelsson, L.E., *The Lord Rose up from Seir: Studies in the History and Traditions of the Negev and Southern Judah* (ConBOT, 25; Lund: Gleerup, 1987).

Bar-Efrat, S., *Narrative Art in the Bible* (JSOTSup, 70; Bible and Literature Series, 17; Sheffield: JSOT Press, 1989).

Bartlett, J.R., 'The Brotherhood of Edom', *JSOT* 4 (1977), pp. 2-27.

—*Edom and the Edomites* (JSOTSup, 77; Sheffield: JSOT Press, 1989).

—'The Land of Seir and the Brotherhood of Edom', *JTS* NS 20 (1969), pp. 1-20.

Berlin, A., *Poetics and Interpretation of Biblical Narrative* (Bible and Literature Series, 9; Sheffield: Almond Press, 1983).

Blank, S.H., 'Studies in Post-Exilic Universalism', *HUCA* 11 (1938), pp. 159-91.

Blum, E., *Die Komposition der Vätergeschichte* (WMANT, 57; Neukirchen–Vluyn: Neukirchener Verlag, 1984).

Boorer, S., 'The Importance of a Diachronic Approach: The Case of Genesis–Kings', *CBQ* 51 (1989), pp. 195-208.

Borger, R., *Babylonisch-assyrische Lesestücke. I. Die Texte in Umschrift. II. Elemente der Grammatik und der Schrift. Glossar. Die Texte in Keilschrift* (AnOr, 54; Rome: Pontificium Institutum Biblicum, 2nd edn, 1979).

Brin, G., 'The Birthright of the Sons of Jacob', *Tarbiz* 48 (1978–79), pp. 1-8 (Hebrew).

Buhl, F. (rev.), *Wilhelm Gesenius' Hebräisches und Aramäisches Handwörterbuch über das Alte Testament* (Leipzig: Verlag Vogel, 13th edn, 1899).

Cross, F.M., 'Reuben, First-Born of Jacob', *ZAW* 100 (1988), pp. 46-65.

Davidson, R., *Genesis 12–50* (CBC; London: Cambridge University Press, 1979).

Dicou, B., *Jakob en Esau, Israël en Edom: Israël tegenover de volken in de verhalen over Jakob en Esau in Genesis en in de grote profetieën over Edom* (Voorburg: Publivorm, 1990).

Dommershausen, W., 'חלל, *hll* I', *ThWAT*, II, pp. 972-81.

Donner, H., 'Adoption oder Legitimation? Erwägungen zur Adoption im Alten Testament auf dem Hintergrund der altorientalischen Rechte', *OrAnt* 8 (1969), pp. 87-119.

Eising, H., *Formgeschichtliche Untersuchung zur Jakobserzählung der Genesis* (Emsdetten: Lechte, 1940).

Eissfeldt, O., *Einleitung in das Alte Testament: Unter Einschluss der Apokryphen und Pseudepigraphen...Entstehungsgeschichte des Alten Testaments* (Neue Theologische Grundrisse; Tübingen: Mohr, 2nd edn, 1956).

—'Stammessage und Novelle in den Geschichten von Jakob und von seinen Söhnen', in *idem, Kleine Schriften* (ed. R. Sellheim and F. Mass; Tübingen: Mohr, 1962), pp. 84-104.

Elliger, K., 'Sinn und Ursprung der priesterlichen Geschichtserzählung', *ZTK* 49 (1952), pp. 121-43. Also in *idem, Kleine Schriften zum Alten Testament* (TBü, 32; Munich: Chr. Kaiser Verlag, 1966).

Eph'al, I., *The Ancient Arabs: Nomads on the Borders of the Fertile Crescent 9th–5th Centuries BC* (Jerusalem: Magnes, 2nd edn, 1984).

Fishbane, M., 'Composition and Structure in the Jacob Cycle (Gen. 25.19–35.22)', *JJS* 26 (1975), pp. 15-38. Cf. also *idem, Text and Texture: Close Readings of Selected Biblical Texts* (The Schocken Jewish Bookshelf; New York: Schocken Books, 1979), pp. 40-62.

—'The Treaty Background of Amos 1:11 and Related Matters', *JBL* 89 (1970), pp. 313-18.

Fokkelman, J.P., *Narrative Art in Genesis: Specimens of Stylistic and Structural Analysis* (Studia Semitica Neerlandica, 17; Assen: Van Gorcum, 1975).

Gunkel, H., *Genesis übersetzt und erklärt* (Göttinger Handkommentar zum Alten Testament; Göttingen: Vandenhoeck & Ruprecht, 5th edn, 1922).

Gunneweg, A.H.J., *Esra* (KAT, 19/1; Gütersloh: Mohn, 1985).

—'Über den Sitz im Leben der sog. Stammessprüche (Gen. 49, Deut. 33, Jud. 5)', *ZAW* 76 (1964), pp. 245-55.

Haller, M., 'Edom im Urteil der Propheten', in K. Budde (ed.), *Vom Alten Testament* (Festschrift Karl Marti; BZAW, 41; Giessen: Töpelmann, 1925), pp. 109-17.

Heintz, J.G., 'בְּאֵר בֹּר', *ThWAT*, I, cols. 500-503.

Helyer, L.R., 'The Separation of Abram and Lot: Its Significance in the Patriarchal Narratives', *JSOT* 26 (1983), pp. 77-88.

Hendel, R.S., *The Epic of the Patriarch: The Jacob Cycle and the Narrative Traditions of Canaan and Israel* (HSM, 42; Atlanta: Scholars Press, 1987).

Humbert, P., 'Die literarische Zweiheit des Priester-Codex in der Genesis', *ZAW* 58 (1940–41), pp. 30-57.

Japhet, S., 'People and Land in the Restoration Period', in G. Strecker (ed.), *Das Land Israel in biblischer Zeit* (Jerusalem Symposium 1981 der Hebräischen Universität und der Georg-August-Universität; Göttinger Theologische Arbeiten, 25; Göttingen: Vandenhoeck & Ruprecht, 1983), pp. 103-25.

Johnson, M.D., *The Purpose of the Biblical Genealogies with Special Reference to the Setting of the Genealogies of Jesus* (SNTSMS, 8; Cambridge: Cambridge University Press, 1969).

Kilian, R., *Die vorpriesterlichen Abrahamsüberlieferungen literarkritisch und traditionsgeschichtlich untersucht* (BBB, 24; Bonn: Peter Hanstein, 1966).

Knauf, E.A., *Ismael: Untersuchungen zur Geschichte Palästinas und Nordarabiens im 1. Jahrtausend v. Chr.* (Abhandlungen des deutschen Palästinavereins; Wiesbaden: Otto Harrassowitz, 2nd edn, 1989).

Koehler, L., and W. Baumgartner, *Hebräisches und aramäisches Lexikon zum Alten Testament neu bearbeitet*, I-III (Leiden: Brill, 1967–83).

Külling, S.R., *Zur Datierung der 'Genesis-P-Stücke' namentlich des Kapitels Genesis XVII* (Kampen: Kok, 1964).

Kutsch, E., ' "Ich will euer Gott sein", *b^erît* in der Priesterschrift', *ZTK* 71 (1974), pp. 361-88.

Laato, A., *Who is Immanuel? The Rise and Foundering of Isaiah's Messianic Expectations* (Åbo: Åbo Academy Press, 1988).

Lang, B., 'kippaer', ThWAT, IV, cols. 303-18.

Lebram, J.C.H., 'Jakob segnet Josephs Söhne: Darstellungen von Genesis XLVIII', OTS 15 (1969), pp. 145-69.

Lemche, N.P., 'Rachel and Leah: Or: On the Survival of Outdated Paradigms in the Study of the Origin of Israel II', SJOT (1988), pp. 39-65.

Lohfink, N., 'Textkritisches zu Gn 17,5.13.16.17', Bib 48 (1967), pp. 439-42.

Löhr, M., Untersuchungen zum Hexateuchproblem. I. Der Priesterkodex in der Genesis (BZAW, 38; Berlin: de Gruyter, 1924).

Long, B.O., The Problem of Etiological Narrative in the Old Testament (BZAW, 108; Berlin: de Gruyter, 1968).

Maag, V., 'Jakob–Esau–Edom', TZ 13 (1957), pp. 418-29.

McEvenue, S., The Narrative Style of the Priestly Writer (AnBib, 50; Rome: Biblical Institute Press, 1971).

Mayes, A.D.H., Deuteronomy: Based on the Revised Standard Version (NCB; Grand Rapids: Eerdmans; London: Marshall, Morgan & Scott, 1981).

Mendelsohn, I., 'A Ugaritic Parallel to the Adoption of Ephraim and Manasseh', IEJ 9 (1959–60), pp. 180-82.

—'On the Preferential Status of the Eldest Son', BASOR 156 (1959), pp. 38-40.

Meyer, E., Die Israeliten und ihre Nachbarstämme: Alttestamentliche Untersuchungen (Halle: Niemeyer, 1906).

Miscall, P.D., 'The Jacob and Joseph Stories as Analogies', JSOT 6 (1978), pp. 28-40.

Myers, J.M., Ezra, Nehemiah: Introduction, Translation and Notes (AB; New York: Doubleday, 1965).

—1 Chronicles: Introduction, Translation and Notes (AB; New York: Doubleday, 1965).

Noth, M., Überlieferungsgeschichte des Pentateuch (Stuttgart: Kohlhammer, 1948).

–Überlieferungsgeschichtliche Studien: Die sammelnden und bearbeitenden Geschichtswerke im Alten Testament (Tübingen: Niemeyer, 2nd edn, 1957).

Ohana, M., 'La polémique judéo–islamique et l'image d'Ismaël dans Targum Pseudo-Jonathan et dans Pirke de Rabbi Eliezer', Augustinianum 15 (1975), pp. 367-87.

Pfeiffer, R.H., Introduction to the Old Testament (New York, London: Harper Bros., 1941).

Rad, G. von, Das erste Buch Mose Genesis übersetzt und erklärt (ATD, 2/4; Göttingen: Vandenhoeck & Ruprecht, 9th edn, 1972).

—Das fünfte Buch Mose Deuteronomium übersetzt und erklärt (ATD, 8; Göttingen: Vandenhoeck & Ruprecht, 1964).

—Die Priesterschrift im Hexateuch literarisch untersucht und theologisch gewertet (BWANT, 65; Stuttgart: Kohlhammer, 1934).

Rahlfs, A. (ed.), Septuaginta, id est Vetus Testamentum graece iuxta LXX interpretes (Stuttgart: Priviligierte Württembergische Bibelanstalt, 1935).

Rendtorff, R., Das überlieferungsgeschichtliche Problem des Pentateuch (BZAW, 147; Berlin: de Gruyter, 1977).

Reymond, P., L'eau, sa vie, et sa signification dans l'Ancien Testament (VTSup, 6; Leiden: Brill, 1958).

Robertson Smith, W., Lectures on the Religion of the Semites: The Fundamental Institutions (ed. S.A. Cook; London: A. & C. Black, 3rd edn, 1927).

Rogerson, J.W., Anthropology and the Old Testament (Oxford: Basil Blackwell, 1978).

—Myth in Old Testament Interpretation (BZAW, 134; Berlin: de Gruyter, 1974).

Rudolph, W., Esra und Nehemia samt 3. Esra (HAT, 20; Tübingen: Mohr, 1949).

—*Joel–Amos–Obadja–Jona: Mit einer Zeittafel von Alfred Jepsen* (KAT, 13/2; Gütersloh: Mohn, 1971).

Schmid, H., 'Ismael im Alten Testament und im Koran', *Judaica* 32 (1976), pp. 76-81, 119-29.

Schneider, K., and E. Stemplinger, 'Alraun', *RAC*, I, pp. 307-10.

Schreiner, J., 'עַיִן *'ajin* מַעְיָן *ma'j ān*', *ThWAT*, VI, cols. 48-56.

Schürer, E., *The History of the Jewish People in the Age of Jesus Christ (175 BC–AD 135)*, I-III (Edinburgh: T. & T. Clark, rev. edn, 1973–87).

Schwarz, E., *Identität durch Abgrenzung: Abgrenzungsprozesse in Israel im 2. vorchristlichen Jahrhundert und ihre traditionsgeschichtlichen Voraussetzungen: Zugleich ein Beitrag zur Erforschung des Jubiläenbuches* (Europäische Hochschulschriften, Reihe XXIII, Theologie, 162; Frankfurt a.M.: Peter Lang, 1982).

Skinner, J., *A Critical and Exegetical Commentary on Genesis* (ICC; Edinburgh: T. & T. Clark, 2nd edn, 1912).

Soden, W. von (rev.), *Akkadisches Handwörterbuch: Unter Benutzung des lexikalischen Nachlasses von Bruno Meissner (1868–1947)*. I. *A–L* (Wiesbaden: O. Harrassowitz, 1965).

Smith, D.L., *The Religion of the Landless: The Social Context of the Babylonian Exile* (Bloomington, IN: Meyer Stone, 1989).

Speiser, E.A., *Genesis: Introduction, Translation, and Notes* (AB; New York: Doubleday, 1964).

Steck, O.H., *Überlieferung und Zeitgeschichte in den Elia-Erzählungen* (WMANT, 20; Neukirchen–Vluyn: Neukirchener Verlag, 1968).

Sternberg, M., *The Poetics of Biblical Narrative: Ideological Literature and the Drama of Reading* (Indiana Literary Biblical Series; Bloomington: Indiana University Press, 1985).

Steuernagel, C., 'Bemerkungen zu Genesis 17', in K. Marti (ed.), *Festschrift Karl Budde* (BZAW, 34; Berlin: Töpelmann, 1920), pp. 172-79.

Syrén, R., *The Blessings in the Targums: A Study on the Targumic Interpretations of Genesis 49 and Deuteronomy 33* (Acta Academiae Aboensis, 64/1; Åbo: Åbo Akademi, 1986).

Thompson, T.L., 'Conflict Themes in the Jacob Narratives', *Semeia* 15 (1979), pp. 5-26.

—*The Historicity of the Patriarchal Narratives: The Quest for the Historical Abraham* (BZAW, 133; Berlin: de Gruyter, 1974).

—*The Origin Tradition of Ancient Israel*. I. *The Literary Formation of Genesis and Exodus 1–23* (JSOTSup, 55; Sheffield: JSOT Press, 1987).

Tsevat, M., 'בְּכֹר', *ThWAT*, I, cols. 643-50.

Van Seters, J., *Abraham in History and Tradition* (New Haven: Yale University Press, 1975).

—'The Problem of Childlessness in Near Eastern Law and the Patriarchs of Israel', *JBL* 87 (1968), pp. 401-408.

Vink, J.G., 'The Date and Origin of the Priestly Code in the Old Testament', *OTS* 15 (1969), pp. 1-144.

Wallis., G., 'Die Tradition von den drei Ahnvätern', *ZAW* 81 (1969), pp. 18-40.

Watts, J.D.W., *The Books of Joel, Obadiah, Jonah, Nahum, Habakkuk and Zephaniah* (CBC; Cambridge: Cambridge University Press, 1975).

Westermann, C., *Genesis 1–11* (BKAT, 1/1; Neukirchen–Vluyn: Neukirchener Verlag, 1974).

—*Genesis 12–36* (BKAT, 1/2; Neukirchen–Vluyn: Neukirchener Verlag, Neukirchen–Vluyn, 1981).

—*Genesis 37–50* (BKAT, 1/3; Neukirchen–Vluyn: Neukirchener Verlag, Neukirchen–Vluyn, 1982).

—'Genesis 17 und die Bedeutung von *berit*', *TLZ* 101 (1976), cols. 161-70.

Wildberger, H., *Jesaja* (BKAT, 10; Neukirchen–Vluyn: Neukirchener Verlag, 1972–82).

Wilson, R.R., *Genealogy and History in the Biblical World* (Yale Near Eastern Researches, 7; New Haven: Yale University Press, 1977).

Wiseman, D.J., *The Alalakh Tablets* (London: British Institute of Archaelogy at Ankara, 1953).

Wolfe, R.E., 'The Editing of the Book of the Twelve', *ZAW* 53 (1935), pp. 90-129.

Wolff, H., *Dodekapropheton*. II. *Joel und Amos* (BKAT, 14/2; Neukirchen–Vluyn: Neukirchener Verlag, 1969).

Zucker, D.J., 'Conflicting Conclusions: The Hatred of Isaac and Ishmael', *Judaism* 39 (1990), pp. 37-46.

INDEXES

INDEX OF REFERENCES

OLD TESTAMENT

INDEX OF AUTHORS